THE COGNOSCENTI'S
GUIDE TO FLORENCE

PRINCETON ARCHITECTURAL PRESS
NEW YORK

The
COGNOSCENTI'S
Guide to
Florence

SHOP and EAT like a FLORENTINE

LOUISE FILI & LISE APATOFF

Published by
Princeton Architectural Press

57 East Seventh Street
New York, New York 10003

Visit our website at www.papress.com.

Editor: Sara E. Stemen.
Book design: Louise Fili and Kelly Thorn. Design assistance:
Nicholas Misani. Cover design: Louise Fili and Spencer Charles.
Photograph on pages 58–59 by Lorenzo Acciai. Special thanks
to: Meredith Baber, Sara Bader, Nicola Bednarek Brower,
Janet Behning, Carey, Carina Cha, Andrea Chlad, Tom Cho,

Barbara Darko, Benjamin
English, Russell Fernandez, Will Foster, Jan Cigliano Hartman, Jan
Haux, Mia Johnson, Diane Levinson, Jennifer Lippert, Katharine
Myers, Jaime Nelson, Rob Shaeffer, Marielle Suba, Kaymar
Thomas, Paul Wagner, Joseph Weston, and Janet Wong
Princeton Architectural Press —Kevin C. Lippert, publisher

Library of Congress Cataloging-in-Publication Data: Fili,
Louise. The cognoscenti's guide to Florence : shop and eat like
a Florentine / Louise Fili and Lise Apatoff. — First edition.
   pages cm. Includes indexes.
   ISBN 978-1-61689-321-7 (paperback)
   I. Apatoff,
   Lise. II. Title.
   TX557.182F555
   2015 381'.
   10945511—dc25
   2014028202

1. Shopping—Italy—Florence—Guidebooks.
2. Restaurants—Italy—Florence—Guidebooks.
3. Florence (Italy)—Guidebooks.
4. Walking—Italy—Florence—Guidebooks.

TABLE OF CONTENTS

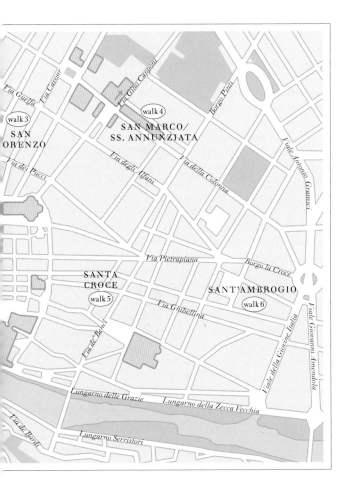

Via Guelfa

Via Cavour

Via Gino Capponi

Borgo Pinti

walk 3

walk 4

SAN
LORENZO

SAN MARCO/
SS. ANNUNZIATA

Viale Antonio Gramsci

Via dei Pucci

Via degli Alfani

Via della Colonna

Via Pietrapiana

Borgo la Croce

SANTA
CROCE

SANT'AMBROGIO

walk 5

walk 6

Via Ghibellina

Via de' Benci

Viale Giovanni Amendola

Viale della Giovine Italia

Lungarno delle Grazie

Lungarno della Zecca Vecchia

Via de' Bardi

Lungarno Serristori

INTRODUCTION

WHILE FLORENTINES BEMOAN THE INFLUX OF THE MEGADESIGNER STORES THAT increasingly globalize their beautiful city, it is nonetheless impressive to see how many family businesses—milliners, bookstores, bakeries, art supply shops, restaurants, woodcarvers, silversmiths, goldsmiths—have continued to flourish for generations. It is heartwarming to hear their stories and see how passionate they are about what they do, and how deeply they love the neighborhoods they live and work in.

For Gabriele and Gherardo Filistrucchi, whose eponymous shop creates custom wigs, it is business as usual since 1720—same name, same building, and two floods later. Or consider artisans like Simone Taddei, who learned the thirty-two-step process of making leather-covered boxes from his father and grandfather—or Ilaria Ballatresi of Dolci & Dolcezze, whose sublime flourless chocolate cake has for decades drawn devotees worldwide.

Whether it is a multigenerational enterprise, or young entrepreneurs who offer a new interpretation of traditional practices, all share a commitment to excellence using time-honored techniques, which is what *The Cognoscenti's Guide to Florence* seeks to celebrate. These are the shops that Florentines have chosen to make part of their daily routines, decade after decade, for good reason.

This book is divided into eight walks, although one of the biggest pleasures of Florence is wandering the winding streets and making your own discoveries. As all exploration requires sustenance, favorite restaurants, caffès, wine bars, and gelaterias are listed at the conclusion of each section. *Buon viaggio e buon divertimento!*

LEGEND

(1) SHOP   (A) FOOD & DRINK

ACCEPTS CREDIT CARDS

DOES NOT ACCEPT CREDIT CARDS

SOME PRACTICAL INFORMATION

HOURS: Most shops in Florence are open from 9 or 10am to 1pm, and 3:30 to 7:30pm, although it is now quite commonplace for more and more shops to remain open all day (*orario continuato*).

In autumn, winter, and spring many shops are closed on Monday mornings. However, in the summer, when schools are not in session (June 15 through the end of August), closings are instead on Saturday afternoons. Few shops are open on Sunday, whatever the season. There was a time not so long ago when the entire country would close down in August (*chiuso per ferie*), but today most shops close only for a week or two. Which week(s) is at the discretion of the shopkeeper, so be prepared for the occasional disappointment.

CHIUSO: Possibly the saddest word in the Italian language, this often appears on shop doors at unanticipated times, and means, simply, *closed*. It can be an indication of a momentary inconvenience, or, when paired with *per sciopero* (strike), it can last the day. (*Torno subito*—back soon—is more hopeful.) Don't despair; by changing course a few degrees you'll undoubtedly stumble onto something equally wonderful elsewhere.

HOLIDAYS: The following dates are religious and state holidays, when offices, banks, and many shops are closed: January 1, January 6, Easter Sunday and Monday, April 25, May 1, June 24, August 15, November 1, December 8, December 25 and 26. Museums are open on a rotating schedule; restaurants often stay open, but call ahead to confirm. Bus service on these days is reduced, following the *festivo* (holiday) schedule, except on May 1 (Workers Day), when public transport stops altogether.

CREDIT CARDS: Many of the shops listed in this book take credit cards, although very few accept American Express. Plan accordingly.

RESTAURANT RESERVATIONS: Although lunch without a reservation is usually not a problem (assuming you arrive by 1pm), a *prenotazione* is recommended for dinner. While it was once a challenge to dine out on a Sunday in Florence, more restaurants are now staying open seven days a week.

SHOPPING ETIQUETTE: Even if you don't have a command of their language, most Italians will appreciate any attempt at communication, no matter how badly you mangle *"Buon giorno, Signora (Signore)"* when entering a shop. Always say thank you when leaving: *"Grazie, Signora (Signore). Buon giorno"* (used in the morning); *"Buona sera"* (anytime from the afternoon on).

THE DE' MEDICI CODE

DURING THE *RISORGIMENTO*, OR "RESUR-GENCE," THE POLITICAL AND SOCIAL PROCESS that unified Italy during the nineteenth century, the city of Florence experienced massive urban renewal. It had become apparent that businesses that were once simply people selling from carts, market stalls, or out of ground floors of family homes were now evolving into the kinds of operations we know today—large and small shops separate from street and home. This posed a distinct municipal problem: how to distinguish business addresses from home addresses. Since it would have been impossible to renumber the entire city, a unique numbering classification was born. As a result, to the dismay and confusion of today's visitors, buildings in Florence operate on two numbering systems. Buildings housing commercial businesses have red numbers, meaning that the number listed in the address is followed by an *r* for *rosso*. The red number on the facade of the building tends to be engraved into a square marble slab, and, with age, appears to be anything but red.

Residential numbers are indicated in black, even though the numbers on the buildings are actually blue, on a white ceramic plate.

While the addresses in this guide are shops and hence should be red, this is not always the case. The red and black numbers do not necessarily correspond (i.e., number 57r can be directly across the street from, say, 100r, and next to a black 31). Moreover, examples of "red" numbers styled in black (see below), and vice-versa, are apt to crop up every now and then.

When all else fails, consult the map at the beginning of each walk. Should you become completely frustrated, a stop at a gelateria or wine bar (also indicated on the map) is a highly recommended and well-deserved diversion.

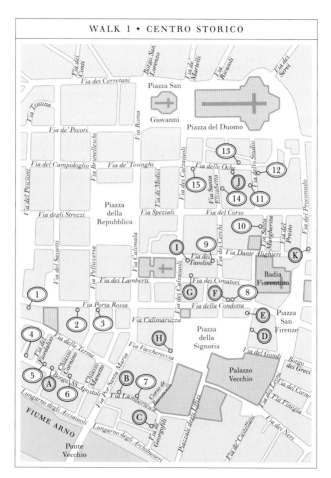

SHOPS

(1) Pampaloni

(2) Passamaneria Valmar

(3) Quercioli e Lucherini

(4) Simone Abbarchi

(5) Tharros Bijoux

(6) Infinity

(7) Laura Nutini

(8) Bizzarri

(9) Falsi Gioielli

(10) Taddei

(11) Zecchi

(12) Pegna

(13) Paperback Exchange

(14) Merceria Samba

(15) Enoteca Alessi

FOOD & DRINK

(A) Mangiafoco

(B) Carapina

(C) 'Ino

(D) Gucci Museo

(E) Vini e Vecchi Sapori

(F) Il Cernacchino

(G) I Due Fratellini

(H) Rivoire

(I) Perché No!

(J) Coquinarius

(K) Alle Murate

PAMPALONI

VIA PORTA ROSSA 99R

▭ ☏ 055 289094 · *pampaloni.com*

MON–SAT 10AM–1:30PM & 3–7:30PM;

CLOSED SUN

PAMPALONI STARTED AS A SILVER SHOP ON THE PONTE VECCHIO IN 1902, WITH THE ENTIRE family living above the store. Now, third-generation Gianfranco continues the tradition of fine crafts-manship in this lovely shop in the *centro*, creating strikingly elegant pitchers, trays, cutlery, candela-bras, frames, decanters, and jewelry in classical as well as contemporary designs. His sleek triangular mirror-finished bowl is in the collection of New York's Museum of Modern Art, while his porcelain dessert plates employ seventeenth-century draw-ings, courtesy of the nearby Uffizi Gallery.

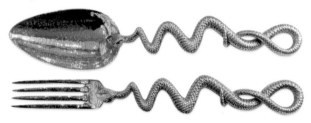

VIA PORTA ROSSA 53R

▭ ☎ 055 284493 · *valmar-florence.com*

MON–FRI 9AM–7:30PM; SAT 10AM–7:30PM;

CLOSED SUN

SINCE THE 1960s, THIS QUINTESSENTIALLY FLOR-
ENTINE, HYPERSOPHISTICATED TRIMMINGS
shop has been the place for nobility (or their
servants) to buy classic *nappe*, or *fiocchi* (tassels),
decorative pillows and buttons, tie backs, ribbons,
edging, tablecloths, and runners, all in a rich
palette of Renaissance colors.

Valmar features intricate appliqués of Florentine
crests for pillows or curtains, which for years have
been handmade with antique fabrics by
the same seamstress. *"Dopo di lei è
la fine. Nessuno sa più come farlo,"*
the owner says, wistfully.
(After she's gone it will
be the end. No one
else knows how
to make them
anymore.)

QUERCIOLI E LUCHERINI

VIA PORTA ROSSA 45R

▭ ☎ 055 292035

MON 3–7PM; TUE–SAT 9AM–1PM & 3–7PM;

CLOSED SUN

I N THE LATE 1800s, TWO FLORENTINES OPENED A *MERCERIA*—A SHOP WHERE THREAD, BUTTONS, embroidery floss, linen, ribbons, and lace were sold, later adding beautiful undergarments to the inventory. The current owner, who took over the shop seventy-five years ago, has continued the tradition, carrying a large assortment of high-quality and unique undergarments for both men and women (while preserving the shop's original carved wooden counter and shelves). The finest camisoles, slips, underwear, socks, and stockings, mostly made in Italy, will make you feel sublime from the inside out.

SIMONE ABBARCHI

BORGO SS. APOSTOLI 16

☎ 055 210552

MON 3:30–7PM; TUE–SAT 10:30AM–1PM &
3:30–7PM; CLOSED SUN & AUG

IN HIS ELEGANTLY APPOINTED SHOP NEAR THE
PIAZZA SANTA TRINITÀ, SIMONE ABBARCHI
creates perfectly tailored handmade shirts for men
and women, as well as suits, jackets, pants, ties, and
scarves, all made to order.

Ranging from the traditional man's dress shirt to
cotton and linen trousers in extravagant shades of
saffron and watermelon, all are produced in his
Fiesole workshop. Allow one month for your order,
which can be shipped worldwide. Signor Abbarchi,
who learned his trade from his *nonno*

(grandfather), travels to
London and New York
City twice a year, fabric
samples in hand, to do
fittings for regular clients.
The extremely helpful staff
speaks English.

THARROS BIJOUX

BORGO SS. APOSTOLI 32R

☎ 055 284126 · *tharros.com*

MON 2:30—7:30PM; TUE–SAT 10AM–1PM &
3:30—7:30PM; CLOSED SUN & AUG

IF YOU EVER HAD A SECRET DESIRE TO DRESS LIKE ELEANORA OF TOLEDO IN HER FAMOUS portrait by Bronzino, head straight to Tharros Bijoux. This beautiful shop tucked into Borgo SS. Apostoli showcases jewelry designs inspired by Renaissance paintings (as well as Victorian, Art Nouveau, and Art Deco time periods). Working with garnets, amethysts, emeralds, sapphires, rubies, and lapis lazuli, Carlo Amato creates dazzling museum reproductions of necklaces, earrings, bracelets, pendants, rings, and brooches that are royalty-worthy, yet very affordably priced. Recently the shop has expanded and now features handmade frames, boxes, and candelabras.

INFINITY

BORGO SS. APOSTOLI 18R

☎ 055 2398405 · *infinityfirenze.com*

MON–SAT 10AM–1PM & 2:30–7PM;

CLOSED SUN

FOR MORE THAN TWENTY-FIVE YEARS, EUGENIO PROVARONI AND HIS AMERICAN WIFE, JANE, have been crafting distinctive handmade leather purses, belts, and wallets in their workshop on Borgo SS. Apostoli.

Drawing from a vast selection of materials—calf, cowhide, sheepskin, suede, fur, deer, elk, snakeskin, alligator, and crocodile—their creations range from classic to more contemporary styles. Choose from hundreds of varieties of buckles, and the Provaronis will make any size and color belt while you wait. Handbags can be made to your specifications (they will happily add that extra zipper or inner pocket) in one to two weeks.

LAURA NUTINI

VIA LAMBERTESCA 8R

▭ ☎ 055 2396563

MON 3:30–7PM; TUE–SAT 9:30AM–1PM & 3:30–7PM;

CLOSED SUN

FOR STYLISH HANDMADE LINENS, NIGHT-GOWNS, LINGERIE, AND HANDKERCHIEFS *"PER signora/bambina/casa,"* as her business card reads, Laura Nutini's shop is not to be missed.

Over the course of decades, Nutini has assembled a group of expert seamstresses who produce handmade, one-of-a-kind creations in the classical tradition. She proudly shows a gossamer nightgown hand-embroidered by an eighty-nine-year-old artisan, which a customer found so enchanting she chose to wear it as a wedding dress. Astonishingly beautiful handsewn monograms are a must-see and are available in a wide variety of styles.

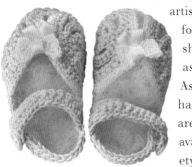

BIZZARRI

ALTHOUGH BIZZARRI SEEMS LIKE AN APT NAME FOR THIS QUIRKY SHOP OF VAGUELY MYSTERIous glass-fronted dark wooden cabinets, it is in fact named after its nineteenth-century founder, *Dottor* Alessandro Bizzarri. Once inside, you will

be mesmerized by the array of test tubes and apothecary jars with neatly typed labels, of spices, extracts, essences, and herbal elixirs. Ask for an *estratto* (extract) of anything from acacia to *zenzero* (ginger) and watch as it is aspirated from a jar using a large calibrated glass straw, then deposited into a tiny glass bottle with an affixed handwritten label. This experience alone is well worth the visit.

FALSI GIOIELLI

VIA DEI TAVOLINI 5R

☎ 055 293296

MON 2:30–7:30PM; TUE–SAT 10AM–7:30PM;

CLOSED SUN

For over twenty-five years, Silvia Fran-ciosi has been adorning Florentines in *falsi gioielli* (fake jewelry)—bracelets, neck-laces, earrings, hairpins, barrettes, and even eyeglass chains—in a riotous spectrum of colors. Created from unusual vintage buttons, crystal, and Plexiglas, they are extremely whimsical and distinctive. While no one will ever mistake this jewelry for precious stones, it is attention-getting nonetheless, and for anywhere between one and sixty euros you can have your own conversation-stopper. Whenever you choose to visit, you will find the staff quietly stringing beads at the back of the shop. Falsi Gioielli has an additional location at Via de' Ginori 34r.

TADDEI

VIA SANTA MARGHERITA 11

▭ ☎ 055 2398960

MON–SAT 8AM–8PM;

CLOSED SUN & AUG

HIDDEN AWAY ON A TINY STREET ACROSS FROM CASA DI DANTE IS THE WORKSHOP OF THE extraordinary artisan Simone Taddei. In the tradition of his father and grandfather, Taddei makes exquisite, highly polished leather boxes in myriad sizes and forms. Working completely alone, Taddei first makes a wooden mold, which is then sanded, covered in calfskin, and stained in a selection of rich colors. From small coin purses to elaborate Louis XIV chests of drawers, Taddei can't ever seem to produce fast enough: "*Questa roba vola dal negozio,*" he laughs, barely looking up from his work table. (This stuff flies out of the store.)

ZECCHI

THERE'S A GOOD CHANCE THAT ANY RESTO-
RATION WORK IN FLORENCE—OR THROUGHOUT
the world, for that matter—has been done using
materials from this renowned art supply store.
Zecchi carries a dazzling selection of the same
beautifully colored dry pigments, gilding supplies,
hand-forged sculpture tools, and paintbrushes once
used by Renaissance masters. For the more modern-
minded artist, a full line of Zecchi's own acrylics,
pastels, and colored pencils is also available. Don't
miss the *tavolozze per i mancini*—wooden palettes
crafted for the left-handed painter, or *camici del
pittore*—classic smocks for the artist or restorer.

PEGNA

VIA DELLO STUDIO 8

☎ 055 282701 · *pegnafirenze.com*

MON–SAT 9:30AM–7:30PM; SUN 11AM–2PM

IT WOULDN'T BE FAIR TO CALL PEGNA A SUPER-MARKET. JUST STEPS FROM THE DUOMO, THIS grand *drogheria/mesticheria/salumeria*, as the sign proclaims, has been serving Florentines and tourists alike since 1860. Don't be fooled by the display of toothbrushes and floor cleaners as you enter; as the store unfolds, a tasteful array of international delicacies, from pâté to fine chocolates, comes into view. The salumeria has excellent prepared foods that will ensure that your last supper—on the plane going home—will be a memorable one.

The cheerful, red-aproned staff will help you with your purchases, which can be delivered.

(13) PAPERBACK EXCHANGE

VIA DELLE OCHE 4R

☎ 055 293460 · *papex.it*

MON–FRI 9AM–7:30PM;

SAT 10AM–1PM & 3:30–7:30PM;

CLOSED SUN & MID-AUG

BILLING THEMSELVES AS THE "ANGLO-AMERICAN BOOKSHOP," PAPERBACK EXCHANGE HAS BEEN a fixture in the English-speaking community since 1979, when Florentine Maurizio Panichi, along with his American wife, Emily Rosner, first opened their doors. Located in an airy space in the *centro*, this shop is the source for thousands of titles in English, many relating to Italy (or more specifically to Florence). The helpful, English-speaking staff can order any book from the United States or Britain within two to three working days. As their name implies, Paperback Exchange also sells secondhand books, in good condition and at reasonable prices.

Poetry readings, literary discussions, children's story hour, and community-related events are scheduled on a regular basis.

MERCERIA SAMBA

VIA SANTA ELISABETTA 10R

✆ 055 215193

MON–FRI 9AM–1PM & 2:30–7PM; SAT 9AM–1PM; CLOSED SUN

BEHIND THE UNASSUMING FACADE OF THIS SEVENTY-FIVE-YEAR-OLD SHOP IS AN IMPOSING wall of buttons in every conceivable color, style, and material, all carefully arranged by hue. Owners Mita and Francesca Villani proudly estimate the number of *bottoni* in their impressive inventory as *"novantanove per cento italiani."* Looking for thread to match a particular fabric? The *merceria* carries 465 different colors. No matter how many people are crowded into the shop (taking a number is advised), Villani *madre e figlia* will spend whatever time is necessary to guarantee that you leave the shop with just the right button.

ENOTECA ALESSI

VIA DELL OCHE 27/29/31R

▭ ☎ 055 214966 · *enotecaalessi.it*

MON–SAT 9AM–7:30PM;

CLOSED SUN

CLOSED SAT & SUN IN AUG

AN ENOTECA IS A SHOP SELLING REGIONAL WINES, ALTHOUGH IN THE CASE OF ALESSI, this is pure understatement. Enter this big and bright third-generation shop, glide through aisles and aisles of colorfully packaged biscotti, *caramelle*, and *cioccolatini* (like the foil-wrapped chocolate "sardines" below), and eventually you will find your way to the back, where the wines are featured (along with extra-virgin olive oils, jams, and aged balsamic vinegars.) In the inviting wine cellar downstairs, you can select from over 2,500 labels and savor your choice with an enticing array of cheeses and *salumi*.

WALK 1 ✦ FOOD & DRINK

(A)
MANGIAFOCO
Borgo SS. Apostoli 26r
💳 ☎ 055 2658170 · *mangiafoco.com*
Lunch & dinner daily · Moderate

A warm welcome and a rosette of prosciutto on *carta di musica* (a paper-thin Sardinian flatbread) will greet you at this intimate wine bar. Husband and wife Francesco and Elisa serve up good pastas, salads, and *salumi*, complemented by house wines and olive oil.

(B)
CARAPINA
Via Lambertesca 18r
 ☎ 055 291128 · *carapina.it*
Tue–Sun noon–9pm; closed Mon · Inexpensive

In the tradition of the best ice cream makers, this tasty little artisan gelateria tucked into a small street "fifty meters from the Ponte Vecchio, Piazza Signoria, and the Uffizi gallery" uses fresh, high-quality, seasonal ingredients to make small batches daily. Ask for the fan-shaped business card, which converts most ingeniously into a cone holder.

(C)
'INO
Via de' Georgofili 37r 💳 ☎ 055 219208
11:30am–4:30pm daily · Moderate

Short for *panino*, here the freshest focaccia meets up with the finest cheeses, cured meats, marinated fish, grilled vegetables, and sauces: saffron, zucchini, truffle, sweet, and spicy. Choose from the expansive menu or the panino of the day, or, better yet, concoct your own. Perch on one of the stools in the back, or take away and enjoy in a picturesque piazza.

GUCCI MUSEO ⓓ

Piazza della Signoria 10 🖩 ☎ 055 75923827
10am–11pm daily (cafe);
Noon–3pm & 7–10pm daily (restaurant) · Moderate

Located on the ground floor of the Gucci museum, this book-store/restaurant/caffè offers sustenance all day, seven days a week, with a repertoire of house-baked bread, composed salads, and traditional pastas, all made with fresh, often organic ingredients. If you are looking for alfresco dining in the Piazza Signoria, this is one of the few places where you will find both a view *and* good food, for lunch or dinner.

VINI E VECCHI SAPORI ⓔ

Via dei Magazzini 3r 🖩 ☎ 055 293045
Mon–Sat 12:30–2:30pm; 7:30–10pm; closed Sun · Moderate

Mamma in the kitchen, *Papà* serving wine and slicing cheese, and quick, competent *figlio* Tommaso waiting tables and handwriting the delicious, daily changing menu (advising *no pizza–no steak–no ice*): all adds up to home cooking at its best. Reserve ahead; this small eatery fills up quickly.

(F) IL CERNACCHINO

Via della Condotta 38r ☒ ☎ 055 294119
9am–7:30pm; closed Sun · Inexpensive

The bustling family-run Cernacchino features an inexpensive, daily changing menu, served quickly, for those on the run: hearty and satisfying panini, salads, soups, risottos, pastas, and house-made cakes. The signature dish is a hollowed crusty roll filled with an overflowing ladleful of sausage and greens, *lampredotto* (tripe), or meatballs. Seating upstairs.

(G) I DUE FRATELLINI

Via dei Cimatori 38r ☒ ☎ 055 2396096
8am–8pm; closed Sun · Inexpensive

When the awning is down, there is no evidence of the name; just look for a lively crowd standing in the street, eating happily. I Due Fratellini serves fresh, delicious panini out of this literal hole in the wall in twenty-seven different varieties. A sandwich and a glass of decent Chianti will set you back only a few euros. Roman numerals on wooden shelves on the exterior wall will help you locate your glass after you set it down.

(H) RIVOIRE

Piazza della Signoria 5 ▭ ☎ 055 214412
8am–midnight; closed Mon · Moderate

For more than one hundred years, this elegant, family-run caffè has been the meeting point for morning cappuccino and pastry, winter afternoon hot chocolate (thick, dark, and topped with freshly whipped cream), celebratory *spumante*, and pre-dinner *aperitivi*. Pastries and prize-winning chocolates are irresistible, and made on the premises. Sit inside or out and take in the beauty of the historic Piazza Signoria.

PERCHÉ NO!
Via dei Tavolini 19r

 ☎ 055 2398969 · *percheno.firenze.it*

11am–10:30pm; closed Tue · Inexpensive

Perché No! (why not!) has been making gelato without coloring, preservatives, or emulsifiers since 1939. All the classic flavors are served, in cups and cones, with additional *panna*, or whipped cream, if desired. According to local lore, Via dei Tavolini was the first street in the *centro* to get postwar streetlights, so that the American soldiers could find their way to this beloved gelateria.

COQUINARIUS
Via delle Oche 11r

☎ 055 2302153 · *coquinarius.it*

12:30–3:30pm & 6:30–10:30pm daily · Moderate

This very comfortable wine bar is ideal for a light meal at just about any time of the day. Eighteen kinds of salads (many of which are vegetarian) are on the menu, as well as crostini, unusual ravioli, and a good selection of wines by the glass. Very friendly service.

ALLE MURATE
Via del Proconsolo 16r

☎ 055 240618 · *allemurate.it*

Lunch & dinner daily · Moderate

This historic building, with frescoes from the thirteenth century, has been beautifully restored as a setting for chef Giovanna Iorio's inspired cuisine. The sixteen-euro lunch is arguably the best deal in Florence: a satisfying four-course meal in a serene atmosphere with attentive service. Keep in mind that the extensive dinner menu is significantly pricier.

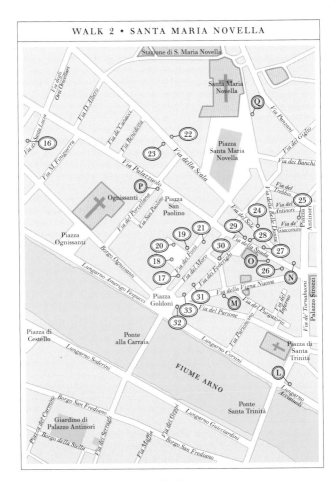

SHOPS

(16) Saskia

(17) Epoca

(18) La Corte

(19) Il Cancello

(20) Tiziana Alemanni

(21) Art & Libri

(22) Officina Profumo Farmaceutica di Santa Maria Novella

(23) Dolceforte

(24) All'Arte del Bronzo

(25) Loretta Caponi

(26) Grevi

(27) Coltelleria Galli

(28) Aprosio & Co

(29) Tip Tap

(30) La Bottega della Frutta

(31) Simone Righi

(32) Anichini

(33) Marioluca Giusti

FOOD & DRINK

(L) Il Borro

(M) Caffè Amerini

(N) Giacosa Caffè (Cavalli Caffè)

(O) Marione

(P) Ostaria dei Centopoveri

(Q) Shake Caffè

16

SASKIA

VIA DI SANTA LUCIA 24R

☎ 055 293291 · *saskiascarpesumisura.com*

MON–FRI 9AM–1PM & 3:30–7PM; SAT 9AM–1PM;

CLOSED SUN

"I HAVE BEEN OBSESSED WITH SHOES EVER SINCE I WAS A LITTLE GIRL IN BERLIN," LAUGHS the redheaded Saskia, whose luminous shop/workshop is filled with magnificently crafted shoes suspended on wires, seemingly dancing through the room. Learning the best of European shoe traditions, she apprenticed with an English-trained Hungarian shoemaker, then with the finest artisan in Florence, opening her eponymous shop on Via di Santa Lucia fourteen years ago.

Want your own *scarpe su misura*? Prepare to invest a little time (and expense). First, a custom wooden last is made. Then, style, color, and materials are chosen. Several fittings and six months later, you will have your own pair of dream shoes, well worth the wait.

While many of Saskia's clients are men, she occasionally makes shoes for women as well.

(17)

EPOCA

VIA DEI FOSSI 6R

🖳 ☎ 055 216698 · *epocavintage.it*

MON—SAT 10AM—7:30 PM; SUN 3:30—7:30PM

(18)

LA CORTE

VIA DEI FOSSI 7R *(inside courtyard)*

🖳 ☎ 335 1252058

MON—SAT 10AM—1PM & 3—7PM;

CLOSED SUN & AUG

(19)

IL CANCELLO

VIA DEI FOSSI 13R

🖳 ☎ 055 2399899 · *antiquariatoilcancello.com*

MON—SAT 10AM—1:30PM & 2:30—7PM;

CLOSED SUN & AUG

FOR THE VINTAGE CLOTHING AFICIONADO, LOOK NO FURTHER THAN VIA DEI FOSSI, where three unique shops showcase French and Italian designer attire for women and men: dresses, suits, hats, shoes, and accessories—from 1900s sequined evening gowns to psychedelic-patterned 1960s minidresses, all in mint condition.

20

TIZIANA ALEMANNI

VIA DEI FOSSI 7R *(inside courtyard)*

▭ ☎ 327 6745143 · *tizianaalemanni.it*

BY APPT

T HE RAVEN-HAIRED, DOE-EYED TIZIANA ALEMANNI CAME TO FLORENCE FROM HER native Sicily, where her family works in the knitting industry, to establish her *sartoria* (dressmaking shop). Alemanni's love affair with fabric is evident: silk, linen, velvet, wool, mohair, cashmere, brocade, lace, iridescent silk, and floating chiffon are used in striking and unusual ways. (Imagine a soft azure velvet dress with knitted sleeves, lined in rose-colored satin.) Everything in the shop—pants, skirts, dresses, suits, jackets, and evening wear—is of her own design and is exquisitely finished with distinctive stitching, buttons, and linings. You may buy off the rack or work with her to fashion your very own dress or evening gown, at comparatively reasonable prices.

"Le donne scoprono quanto sono veramente belle con i miei vestiti," observes the *sarta.* (Women discover how beautiful they really are in my clothes.)

21

ART & LIBRI

VIA DEI FOSSI 32R

☎ 055 264186 · *artlibri.it*

MON–SAT 9:30AM–1PM & 3:30–7:30PM

CLOSED SUN & TWO WEEKS IN AUG

ALFREDO LUPI HAS SOLD BEAUTIFUL ART BOOKS FROM THIS SPACIOUS, BRIGHTLY LIT SHOP for close to twenty years. In addition to an extensive international inventory of new and antiquarian books on fine arts, photography, interior design, and architecture, Art & Libri also carries a large selection of monographs and catalogs, as well as books on the history of Florence. The knowledgeable and helpful staff speaks English and can special order publications from around the world. You can browse to your heart's content at this shop, which also has branches in Rome and Paris.

22

OFFICINA PROFUMO FARMACEUTICA DI SANTA MARIA NOVELLA

VIA DELLA SCALA 16

▭ ☎ 055 216276 · *smnovella.it*

MON—SUN 9AM—8PM

YOU MAY HAVE SEEN THESE EXQUISITELY PACK-AGED SOAPS, LOTIONS, AND POTIONS IN OTHER locales, but a trip to the source is an experience not to be missed. Enter this cool, dark, seventeenth-century temple of *profumi* and you will find your-self transported to a sensuous other dimension.

A short distance from the church and piazza of the same name, Officina Profumo Farmaceutica di Santa Maria Novella is one of the world's oldest pharmacies. The Dominican fathers, who first arrived in Florence in 1221, collected herbs from the courtyard garden to create their own medicines for the monastery's infirmary and then opened to the public in 1612.

A black-jacketed tribunal of sales clerks will assist you with the endless and enticing inventory of the Officina's essences and perfumes, which are

still prepared according to the original formulas developed in 1500 for Caterina de' Medici. Printed lists of the *farmacia*'s offerings are available in every imaginable language and will  guide you to a host of discoveries: Aceto dei Sette Ladri (Vinegar of the Seven Thieves), whose recipe dates back to 1600, is still a favorite antidote for fainting spells. Acqua Antisterica, today sold as Acqua di Santa Maria Novella, for "a sedative and antispasmodic effect," was created by Fra'Angiolo Marchissi in 1614. The Acqua di Rose, a tonic to soothe red eyes, and the Pasta di Mandorle, a fragrant almond hand cream, are as beautiful as they are effective.

In honor of the four hundredth anniversary of the farmacia, the space has greatly expanded to include the restored fourteenth-century frescoed chapel, while the offerings have broadened to include beautifully packaged chocolates, biscotti, fruit preserves, teas, honeys, and liqueurs.

23

DOLCEFORTE

VIA DELLA SCALA 21R

☎ 055 219116 · *dolceforte.it*

MON & WED–SAT 10AM–1PM & 3:30–7:45PM;

TUE 3:30–7:45PM; CLOSED SUN

AFTER A TRIP TO THE HOLY SANCTUARY OF *PRO-FUMI* AT SANTA MARIA NOVELLA, INDULGE your senses further at Dolceforte. In winter, this sweet shop features fine chocolates (primarily from Tuscany). Purists will delight in Tuscan favorites such as Amedei (from an area outside of Pisa dubbed the "Valley of Chocolate") or an oversized tube of Gianduioso—the seductively squeezable hazelnut-chocolate cream. After Easter, when the temperature is less favorable for chocolate, marzipan makes an appearance, as do the finest artisan pastas, biscotti, and a selection of delicious jams and pestos from the best producers in Tuscany, Liguria, and Sicily.

24

ALL'ARTE DEL BRONZO

VIA DEL SOLE 13R

▭ ☎ 055 283518 · *rafanellibronzisti.it*

TUE–SAT 10AM–1PM & 3–7PM;

CLOSED SUN, MON & AUG

NONNO RAFANELLI STARTED HIS FOUNDRY IN A SMALL TOWN NORTH OF FLORENCE SIXTY-four years ago, smelting and producing bronze and brass door handles, drawer pulls, hooks, and ornaments for furniture. He probably never could have imagined that his sons, and his sons' sons, would have carried on the business and opened a charming, expansive store on Via del Sole. Here, in addition to the original classical ornaments, this new generation of Rafanellis produces bed frames, lamps, chandeliers, coatracks, and door buzzers, supplying these expertly crafted historical designs to clients all over the world.

H7
68,00

H8
73,00

H9
38,00

H10
68,00

H11
71,00

H12
56,00

H15
58,00

H16
45,00

25

LORETTA CAPONI

PIAZZA ANTINORI 4R

☎ 055 213668 · *lorettacaponi.com*

MON 3:30−7:30PM;

TUE−SAT 9AM−1PM & 3:30−7:30PM;

CLOSED SUN; CLOSED SAT AFTERNOON IN AUG

ELITE FLORENTINES HAVE BEEN ENHANC-ING THEIR HOMES WITH LORETTA CAPONI'S creations since 1966. Although best known for her delicate embroidery, she also makes beautiful nightgowns and bathrobes in a variety of colors, styles, and lush fabrics. This enchanting space, with highly polished floors and rose-garland-frescoed ceilings, features racks of lovely lace christening gowns, flower girl dresses, gossamer blouses, beribboned hats, and smocked outfits. The signature embroidery graces tablecloths, pillows, bedspreads, napkins, and guest towels. Caponi tells of one client who sent over a porcelain dinner plate to have its wisteria design replicated on an oversized tablecloth and napkins. Then there was the rush order for a golf-themed tablecloth that "had us embroidering blades of green grass late into the night."

26

GREVI

THIS TINY, FOURTH-GENERATION *CAPPELLERIA* IS A CELEBRATION OF STYLISH HATS FOR MEN, women, and children, all woven and crocheted by master craftsmen in Grevi's workshop in nearby Signa since 1875. Wool, felt, velvet, straw, organza, and cotton are expertly crafted with fanciful flowers, appliqués, and embroidery into delicious works of art in a spectrum of colors, according to the season. Delicate bonnets, gloves, and *passate* (hairbands) for children are hard to resist. Equally delightful handbags and fans are also available. The friendly staff speaks English and will be happy to ship your purchases home for you.

27

COLTELLERIA GALLI

VIA DELLA SPADA 26R

▭ ☎ 055 282410

MON–SAT 9AM–1PM & 3–7:30PM; CLOSED SUN & AUG

"*MI PUOI METTERE NEL LIBRO SE NON MI DA PIÙ LAVORO,*" SAYS FILIPPO GALLI. (YOU can put me in the book as long as I don't get any more work.) His tiny shop houses an encyclopedic collection of knives and scissors of every possible type and size. Galli sharpens utensils for most residents of the neighborhood, and he supplies restorers, tailors, barbers, chefs, bookbinders, gardeners, and manicurists citywide. Following Italian tradition, Galli carries the finest shaving supplies: soaps, creams, brushes, and razors, along with toothpaste and toothbrushes. While browsing the shop, you are bound to observe any number of locals dropping in to buy a potato peeler. "*Il migliore che c'è,*" they say. (The best there is.) They may well be right.

28

APROSIO & CO

FOR OVER TWENTY YEARS, ORNELLA APROSIO HAS CREATED BREATHTAKING DESIGNS OF delicately woven glass jewelry and accessories. A team of experienced artisans works with minute Murano glass beads and Bohemian crystals, from Venice and the Czech Republic, respectively, to create exquisite earrings, bracelets, necklaces, brooches, purses, gloves, and hats, using traditional techniques such as weaving, crochet, needlepoint, and knitting. Aprosio, who draws her inspiration from nature, uses themes of flowers, fruits, insects, and the sea, offering a contemporary interpretation of an ancient craft. If you don't happen to find the particular color or size that you are looking for, your bauble can be made to order.

29

TIP TAP

VIA DELLA SPADA 50R

▭ ☎ 055 2398488

MON 3:30–7:30PM;

TUE–SAT 10AM–1PM & 3:30–7:30PM;

CLOSED SUN

TIP TAP KEEPS THE FEET OF LOCAL *BAMBINI* IN STYLE FROM BIRTH TO SIZE EIGHT (WHICH means that some lucky grown-ups can shop here as well). Every pair of beautiful shoes in this sliver of a shop on Via della Spada is made in Italy. The extensive selection includes lace-ups, slip-ons, sandals, boots, and slippers. All of the classic styles are kept in constant supply, and, in addition, the iconic Friulane—handmade velvet slippers from

the Friuli region in the north—are available in a selection of colors. Tip Tap also features colorful, buttery-soft cashmere scarves and a line of charmingly classic hats made from straw and felt.

(30) LA BOTTEGA DELLA FRUTTA

VIA DEI FEDERIGHI 31R

☎ 055 2398590

MON–SAT 8:30AM–7:30PM;

CLOSED SUN & AUG;

CLOSED SAT AFTERNOON IN JUN AND JUL

LETI AND HER HUSBAND, FRANCESCO, HAVE BEEN SATISFYING THE NEIGHBORHOOD APPE-tite for thirty-three years with this little shop of culinary delights, where a bicycle parked outside greets customers with a basket of fresh flowers and produce of the day. Inside, you will find *il meglio di Firenze:* quite simply, "the best" in fresh seasonal fruits and vegetables, artisan cheeses, *salumi*, and fragrant crusty bread that the couple routinely picks up from their own baker on the way to the shop each morning. The overflowing antique shelves beautifully showcase artisan pastas, biscotti, jams, sauces, chocolates, olives, crackers, artisan beers, and carefully selected wines (along with the occasional Italian proverb). Everything you need for a gourmet picnic can be found here—or ask Leti to prepare a sure-to-be-appreciated gift basket.

31

SIMONE RIGHI

VIA DEI FEDERIGHI 7R

▭ ☎ 055 211015 · *simonerighi.it*

MON 9:30AM–1PM;

TUE–SAT 9:30AM–1PM & 3:30–7:30PM;

CLOSED SUN & AUG

A GENTLEMAN COULD WALK INTO THIS ELE-
GANT SHOP STARK NAKED AND LEAVE
perfectly dressed, from head to toe, for any occasion. For more than thirty years, Simone Righi
has delighted in dressing his customers with fine
jackets, shirts, vests, sweaters, coats, gloves, hats,
scarves, shoes, socks, and ascots in luscious fabrics
and subtle colors. The dapper Signor Righi, always
impeccably attired, serves as the best advertising
for this shop. He draws from the two great Italian
tailoring traditions, Neapolitan and Florentine,
embracing elegance and ease in fashion.

Every item of clothing can be ordered in any
size, color, and material, with specifications for
lining, stitching, and trim. "*Ognuno ha la sua
storia,*" Righi purrs. (Every man has his own story.
I am just here to help realize his potential.)

32

ANICHINI

VIA DEL PARIONE 59R

☎ 055 284977 · *anichini.net*

MON 3:30—7:30PM;

TUE—SAT 9:30AM—1:30PM & 3:30—7:30PM;

CLOSED SUN

TO DRESS A CHILD WELL IS THE ITALIAN WAY OF SHOWING LOVE. *BAMBINI* SHOULD BE AS fashionable as their parents! From 1912 the Anichini name was synonymous with beautiful camisoles. They later started outfitting children, and today, a fourth generation carries on the tradition. This charming shop (with stuffed bears and rabbits peeking out everywhere) stocks alluring Italian and French designs for newborns up to twelve-year-olds. Most of the sweaters, coats, jack-ets, party dresses, shirts, pants, hats, headbands, and socks, all in natural mate-rials, are produced locally, specifically for the shop, and can be special ordered and shipped worldwide.

33

MARIOLUCA GIUSTI

VIA DELLA VIGNA NUOVA 88R

☎ 055 2399527 · *mariolucagiusti.com*

TUE–SAT 10AM–1:30PM & 3–7PM; SUN & MON 3–7PM;

CLOSED SAT & SUN IN AUG

SCION OF A STORIED FLORENTINE FAMILY, MARIOLUCA GIUSTI WORKS WITH A JEWEL-toned acrylic that looks and feels astonishingly like glass, fashioning goblets, pitchers, ice buckets, salad bowls, cake stands, serving trays, candlesticks, oil and vinegar cruets, lamp bases and shades, and even wastebaskets in a kaleidoscopic array of colors. Should you happen to find yourself a guest at the chic Tuscan seaside resort Il Pellicano, or the Philippe Starck–designed Mama Shelter in Paris, you will most likely be sipping wine from a Giusti

goblet. Better yet, visit this shop on the Via della Vigna Nuova and select from twelve different styles (from Victoria and Albert to La Dolce Vita) in vibrant shades of red, royal blue, green, purple, fuchsia, silver, gold, and amber.

(L) ## IL BORRO
Lungarno Acciaiuoli 80r ▭ ☎ 055 290423
10am–10pm daily; closed Mon in winter · Moderate

Il Borro is the Ferragamo estate restaurant, serving light, imaginative dishes using produce from their own gardens as well as other small local farms. Open all day for breakfast, lunch, and dinner. Sit in the back and watch the chef make his magic in the inviting glassed-in kitchen.

(M) ## CAFFÈ AMERINI
Via della Vigna Nuova 63r ▭ ☎ 055 284941
Breakfast, lunch & aperitivi *daily until 9:30pm · Moderate*

Don't even *think* of asking for a menu. "*Il menù è la vetrina,*" greets your host. In other words, choose from the glass case, place your order with the chic, black-shirted young man behind the counter, find a seat, eat, pay. Amerini is known for its fast service, fresh *insalatone* (big salads), and panini, but especially for the glamorous clients, many of whom are impeccably dressed shop clerks from nearby Via de' Tornabuoni, eating lunch with their sunglasses on. You'll want to stay all day for the nonstop parade of fashion.

(N) ## GIACOSA CAFFÈ (CAVALLI CAFFÈ)
Via della Spada 10r ▭ ☎ 055 2776328
Mon–Sat 8am–8:30pm; Sun 12:30–8pm · Moderate

"Sweets, pastries, wines and spirits, restaurant, tea room, chocolate factory. Licensed furnishers to the Royal family since 1815." So reads the original letterhead for the famed Giacosa Caffè. When designer Roberto Cavalli bought the building in 2002, the locals protested so loudly that the caffè was kept open. Although now in a smaller, more modern space, Giacosa has maintained its high standards for cappuccino, pastries, sandwiches, light lunch, and *aperitivi*. This is still the place where the Florentine elite meet, along with those who appreciate a good espresso and people watching.

MARIONE

Via della Spada 27r 📠 ☎ 055 214756
Lunch & dinner; closed Sun · Inexpensive/Moderate
Hanging prosciuttos welcome you upon entering this warm, lively restaurant, where locals come for good homemade pastas and *ribollita* (a hearty Florentine bread-and-vegetable soup). Lunch service is cordial albeit rushed; arrive early.

OSTARIA DEI CENTOPOVERI

Via Palazzuolo 31r 📠 ☎ 055 218846
Lunch & dinner daily until 11pm · Inexpensive
The daily-changing, ten-euro lunch menu, featuring two courses plus wine and water, is one of the best deals in town. Pizzas and a large à la carte menu are also available. Dinner offers a more complete (and more expensive) selection, as well as pizzas. No pizza at lunch Saturday or Sunday.

SHAKE CAFFÈ

Via degli Avelli 2r (east edge of
Piazza Santa Maria Novella) 📠 ☎ 055 295310
7am–8pm daily (until 11pm in Jul & Aug) · Inexpensive
A healthy alternative for breakfast or a light meal, Shake Caffè makes refreshing smoothies and juices using fresh fruits and vegetables, and is one of the few caffès to offer rice, soy, and almond milks. Enjoy tasty wraps, salads, pastries, and gelato while sitting outside at no extra charge.

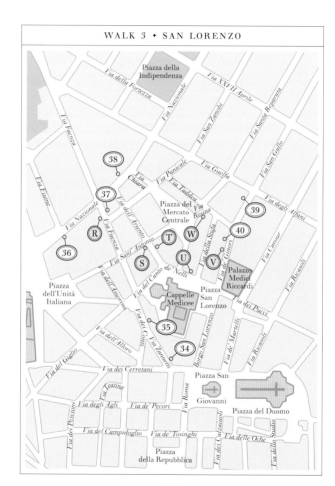

SHOPS

(34) Penko

(35) Ceramiche Ricceri

(36) Alinari

(37) Alice's Masks
Art Studio

(38) Mondo Albion

(39) Maselli

(40) Fiori del Tempo

FOOD & DRINK

(R) Lobs

(S) Antica Pasticceria
Sieni

(T) Casa del Vino

(U) Sergio Gozzi

(V) Le Botteghe di
Leonardo

(W) Pepò

PENKO

VIA ZANNETTI 14R

▭ ☎ 055 211661 · *paolopenko.com*

TUE–SAT 9:30AM–1:30PM & 3:30–7:30PM;

CLOSED SUN & MON

RING THE BUZZER AT THE DOOR OF THIS SHOP, AND THE LOWERED HEAD OF EACH family member will look up from a fine piece being handcrafted in gold, silver, or precious stones. Earrings, necklaces, medallions, and unique decorative pieces are made with expertise, using antique tools. Penko is known for a signature "Florentine ring": a lacy yellow- and white-gold band incised by hand so it sparkles. The necklaces of small hammered gold rings are from an ancient Etruscan design. Purchase a reproduction of the famous gold florin of 1252, and they will mint it for you while you watch. *Proprietario* Paolo Penko is eloquent and knowledgeable, making each visit even more memorable.

35

CERAMICHE RICCERI

VIA DEI CONTI 14R

▭ ☎ 055 291296 · *riccericeramica.com*

MON–SAT 10AM–1PM & 3–7PM

CLOSED SUN & PART OF AUG

POPPIES, SUNFLOWERS, GRAPES, AND LEMONS ALL COME TO LIFE IN AN EXPLOSION OF color in this diminutive shop. For eight generations, the Ricceri family has produced at their workshop in the Chianti area these lovely hand-molded and hand-painted pitchers, plates, bowls, trays, cups, vases, and lamps in a variety of shapes and sizes with lead-free glazes. Choose from Florentine Renaissance, medieval, and botanical designs. Ricceri is happy to take special and personalized orders. The shop's guaranteed shipping policy will spare you the effort of trying to cram a set of dishes into your luggage, and ensure that your ceramics will arrive safely to grace your table.

36

ALINARI

LARGO ALINARI 15

▭ ☎ 055 23951 · *alinari.com*

MON & FRI 9AM–1PM;

TUE, WED, THU 9AM–1PM & 2–6PM;

CLOSED SAT & SUN

FOUNDED IN 1852, FRATELLI ALINARI IS THE OLDEST PHOTOGRAPHIC ARCHIVE IN THE world. Housed in the shop along with the collection are books, exhibition catalogs, postcards, tote bags, calendars, magnets, notebooks, notepads, and bookmarks as well as matted and framed prints, all culled from the massive archive of beautiful black-and-white images—from iconic portraits to vivid landscapes, from Antonioni to Zimbabwe. Prints (in either black-and-white or sepia) can be custom ordered from the original glass-plate negatives.

Note: Alinari is easy to miss. Largo Alinari is at the intersection of Via Nazionale and Via Fiume, one block from the Piazza della Stazione. Look for number 15. If you are very tall or alert, you may spot a sign above the building entrance. Walk straight back to the courtyard, and look for the shop on the right.

37

ALICE'S MASKS
ART STUDIO

VIA FAENZA 72R

▭ ☎ 055 287370 · *alicemasks.com*

MON—SAT 9AM—1PM & 3:30—7:30PM; CLOSED SUN

N O, YOU HAVEN'T JUST BEEN AIRLIFTED INTO VENETIAN CARNEVALE. AGOSTINO DESSI, the Sardinian-born artist, has been designing and producing papier-mâché masks in his Florence studio for over three decades. This shop hosts an ever-changing parade of devils and angels, suns and moons, rabbits, cats, birds, camels, harlequins, and Pinocchios; a face to suit your every mood. In 1997, *Professor* Dessi was joined by his daughter Alice, who works alongside her father at the back of the shop and conducts a mask-making workshop during the last week of every month. The duo's internationally known masks are used for theater, film, and, of course, Carnevale in Venice.

38

MONDO ALBION

VIA NAZIONALE 121R

✉ ☎ 055 282451 · *mondoalbion.it*

MON–SAT 10AM–1PM & 3–7PM;

CLOSED SUN & AUG

IN A CITY OVERRUN WITH SHOE STORES, MONDO ALBION IS WITHOUT QUESTION THE most unusual. With his long white beard and eclectic wardrobe, Signor Albion has been designing handmade shoes that defy description for over half a century. While his *calzaiolo* works at his craft at the front of the shop, the affable Albion holds court amid hundreds of distinctive pairs of colorful sandals, pumps, platforms, and boots—some perfect as Halloween attire, others quite wearable and comfortable. Still others are emblazoned with his distinctive prose, which also happens to appear on whatever he is wearing that day. Example: *"Meglio camminando, genio permettendo."* (Better walking, genius permitting.) No matter what your experience, you are likely to leave the shop with a unique pair of shoes (gondola-shaped slippers, anyone?) and an unforgettable tale to go with them.

39

MASELLI

VIA DE' GINORI 51R

▭ ☎ 055 282142 · *cornicimaselli.it*

MON–SAT 9AM–1PM & 3:30–7:30PM;

CLOSED SUN & AUG

FROM THE AGE OF FOURTEEN, GABRIELE MASELLI KNEW THAT HE WANTED TO MAKE FRAMES, but his father, a seller of antique prints, insisted that his son finish school instead. By the time Maselli graduated, he was a specialist in carving and gilding wooden frames. His intimate shop is filled floor to ceiling with more than six hundred designs. He can copy, repair, or find the perfect solution for any picture or object that needs a flawless setting. In addition, he does meticulous restoration work

for churches (the Vatican included), museums (the Uffizi), and private collections, where he finds that "so often the frame is a work of art in itself." In Maselli's case, this is most certainly true.

40

FIORI DEL TEMPO

VIA DE' GINORI 27R

▭ ☎ 055 217639

MON—SAT 10AM—2PM; 3:30—7:30PM;

CLOSED SUN

FRANCESCO DAIDDA STARTED GOLDSMITHING SCHOOL AS A TEENAGER AND OPENED HIS first shop soon thereafter. Using gold-leafed silver, river pearls, and semiprecious stones such as coral, amethyst, malachite, tiger's eye, lapis lazuli, quartz, and jade, Daidda creates unique necklaces, rings, and pins, although earrings are the true standouts. In addition to his reproductions of antique and Art Deco pieces, he has also created a delightful series of contemporary resin pieces in classical shapes using vivid color combinations. His workshop is directly behind the antique wooden counter in this vaulted-ceilinged shop, which allows him to take special requests and orders on the spot. Ask for his handwritten business card, which is adorned with a crimson spot of sealing wax.

LOBS
Via Faenza 75r 📋 ☎ 055 212478
Lunch & dinner daily · Moderate

Fresh fish, deliciously and simply prepared, is a pleasant departure from typical Florentine carnivore fare at Lobs (as in *lobster*). A welcoming glass of Prosecco, maritime decor, and illuminated globes on the tables add to the charm. Good pastas are served at lunch.

ANTICA PASTICCERIA SIENI
Via Sant'Antonio 54r
📋 ☎ 055 213830 · *pasticceriasieni.it*
7:30am–7:30pm daily · Inexpensive

Since 1909 this corner store has been serving coffee to the workers operating the stands at the nearby San Lorenzo market. Pastries, sandwiches, and ample seating. Try the *cantucci*, the classic Tuscan biscotti, with your espresso.

CASA DEL VINO
Via dell'Ariento 16r
📋 ☎ 055 215609 · *casadelvino.it*
Mon–Fri 9:30am–3:30pm & 5:30–8pm; Sat 10am–3:30pm;
closed Sun · Inexpensive

A comfortable space with dark, carved wooden cabinetry and marble floors, Gianni Migliorini's classic wine bar is a lively refuge in the teeming San Lorenzo market. For a quick lunch or *aperitivo*, stand up at the bar and choose from a dozen reds or whites, or try the house Prosecco. Order from the extensive selection of delicious four-euro panini and crostini, and get a recommendation for a wine to pair with it.

SERGIO GOZZI

Piazza San Lorenzo 8r 🖶 ☎ 055 281941
Lunch & dinner daily · Moderate

Since 1915 generations of Gozzi have continued with the
same winning no-frills formula: the satisfying fare on their
daily changing menu (choices of *primi*, *secondi*, and *contorni*)
is served quickly, with banter. The citations on the door and
daily crowd of locals attest to Gozzi's bravura.

LE BOTTEGHE DI LEONARDO

Via de' Ginori 21r 🖶 ☎ 055 285052
Nov–May: 12:30–8:30pm; Jun–Oct: noon–11:30pm;
closed Sun · Inexpensive

Leonardo is passionate about gelato-making and uses only
the finest ingredients: milk from the mountain dairies of
Trentino, Domori chocolate from Ecuador, pistachios from
Bronte in Sicily. Can't decide? Opt for "Contemplation":
three cups of different flavors in an elegant carry-out box.

PEPÒ

Via Rosina 4/6r 🖶 ☎ 055 283259 · *pepo.it*
Lunch & dinner daily · Moderate

For the perfect *spaghetti al dente* with a good, simple sauce of
fresh tomatoes, garlic, and basil, Pepò never disappoints: their
affordable lunch and dinner, served by a cheerful staff amid
a decor that is both modern and rustic, has made this spot
a favorite among locals. The daily changing menu features
excellent pastas, soups, and main courses, using the freshest ingredients from the nearby Mercato Centrale. Try the
fried vegetables (artichokes or porcini mushrooms, depend-
ing on the season), *spaghetti alle vongole*, or, if you are feeling
adventurous, egg noodles with wild boar sauce.

Piazza della
Indipendenza

Via Venezia

Giardino di
San Clemente

Via XXVII Aprile

(b)

Via San Gallo

Via Cavour

Via La Pira

Giardino
dei Semplici

Via G: Capponi

Via P.A. Micheli

Via Santa Reparata

(46)

Piazza
San Marco

(a)

(47)

Via Guelfa

Via C. Battisti

SS. Annunziata

Galleria
dell'
Accademia

Via Taddea

(48)

Via Cavour

Via degli Alfani

Piazza
della
SS. Annunziata

Museo
Archeologico

Via della Sigla

Via de' Ginori

Palazzo
Medici
Riccardi

Via Ricasoli

(X) (Y)

(Z)

(45)

Via della Colonna

Via Laura

(44)

B.S. Lorenzo

Via de'
Gori

Via de' Martelli

(41)

Via dei Pucci

(43)

(42)

Via dei Servi

Via del Castellaccio

Giardino
del Museo
Archeologico

Via degli Alfani

Via M. Bufalini

Via della Pergola

Giardino
di Palazzo
Caccinii

Piazza San
Giovanni

Piazza del Duomo

Via dell'Oriuolo

Via Sant'Egidio

Borgo Pinti

Via Fiesolana

Via Roma

Via dei Calzaioli

Via dello Studio

Via del Proconsolo

Borgo degli Albizi

SHOPS

(41) Scriptorium   (46) Pugi

(42) Alba   (47) Maison Rouge

(43) Bartolini   (48) Dreoni

(44) Farmacia SS. Annunziata

(45) Street Doing

FOOD & DRINK

(X) Carabé   (a) Pugi

(Y) Arà   (b) Ristorante da Mimmo

(Z) Robiglio

SCRIPTORIUM

VIA DEI PUCCI 4 *(inside courtyard)*

▭ ☎ 055 211804 · *scriptoriumfirenze.com*

MON–FRI 9:30AM–7:30PM; SAT 9:30AM–1PM;

CLOSED SUN

A PASSION FOR THE ART OF WRITING IS IMME-DIATELY APPARENT IN THIS CHARMING shop not far from the convent of San Marco, where Dominican monks toiled at their illuminated manuscripts. This ancient craft is still alive and well at Scriptorium, which sells everything for the lover of hand-made books and calligraphy. From their own signature inks, pens, sealing wax, and blank books to fine leather-covered boxes to personalized stationery stamped in gold, Scriptorium has everything for the modern-day scribe. *Contenitori libri* (hollowed-out leather books to hide anything from jewelry to a mini-bar) are particularly gift-worthy.

[112]

Scriptorium

Firenze

42

ALBA

VIA DEI SERVI 27R

▭ ☎ 055 287754 · *abbigliamento-lavoro.it*

MON–FRI 9:30AM–1:30PM & 3–7PM;

SAT 9:30AM–1:30PM;

CLOSED SUN; CLOSED SAT IN JUL & AUG

WITH THE MEMORABLE SLOGAN *"VESTE IL TUO LAVORO"* (DRESS FOR YOUR JOB), THIS uniform store has been stylishly outfitting Florentine professionals since 1956. Together with neighbor Bartolini (page 116), Alba can help you look and cook just like a bona fide Italian chef, outfitting you in toques (cloth or paper), neckerchiefs, jackets, pants (checked or striped), and clogs. Or consider their classic waiter's and maid's uniforms, aprons, and vests. Or medical attire. All styles are durable and machine washable, are available either ready-to-wear or made-to-order, and can be personalized with Alba's expert hand embroidery.

The shop also features service gloves for butlers, which can be made to order in a range of styles and fabrics.

43

BARTOLINI

VIA DEI SERVI 72R

☎ 055 291497 · *dinobartolini.it*

MON–SAT 10AM–7PM;

CLOSED SUN

IF A KITCHEN GADGET EXISTS, EXPECT TO FIND IT AT BARTOLINI. FOR OVER SEVENTY-FIVE years, this store has been the source for all things for the professional and home cook: heavy-bottomed copper pots and pans, knives, espresso machines, crystal (more than 200 styles of wine and drinking glasses), and cutlery (well over 130 services, from the most elegant to everyday). This spacious shop offers a dizzying array of wares for every taste and budget. If you happen to be interested in a pasta machine, you can choose from the popular Imperia brand found in most Italian homes or the more artisan *chitarra* (resembling guitar strings) for hand-cut pasta. Bartolini will ship worldwide.

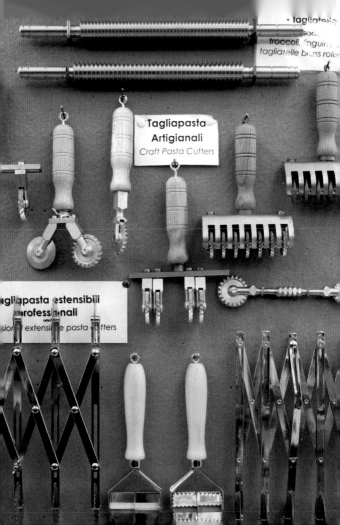

(44) FARMACIA SS. ANNUNZIATA

VIA DEI SERVI 80R

📠 ☎ 055 210738 · *farmaciassannunziata1561.it*

MON—FRI 9AM—1PM & 4—7:30PM; SAT 9AM—1PM;

CLOSED SUN & AUG

IN 1561 HERBALIST AND CHEMIST DOMENICO DI VINCENZO BRUNETTI MOVED HIS SHOP TO a beautiful vaulted space on Via dei Servi. Today, the same sculpted, dark wooden cabinets of the Farmacia SS. Annunziata are still stocked with the *farmacia*'s exclusive line of natural products, all handmade using the original formulas in simple yet classic signature black-and-white packaging. Choose from a delectable menu of skin- and hair-care products for men, women, and children: rosemary and sage soap, calendula exfoliating cream, almond bath gel, sage toothpaste, ginkgo hair conditioner, carrot suntan oil, bilberry aftershave, and chamomile baby shampoo. An enticing fragrance line, from *agrumi* (citrus) to *vaniglia di Madagascar*, completes the selection.

45

STREET DOING

VIA DEI SERVI 88R

☎ 055 5381334 · *streetdoingvintage.it*

MON 2:30–7:30PM; TUE–SAT 10:30AM–7:30PM;
CLOSED SUN

A VERITABLE MUSEUM OF VINTAGE FASHION, STREET DOING FEATURES ROOM AFTER ROOM of an eclectic mix of some of the best examples of classic Florentine fashion heroes—Emilio Pucci, Gucci, Roberto Cavalli, and Salvatore Ferragamo, as well as French and American designers. A seemingly endless supply of stylish shoes, boots, purses, scarves, belts, evening gowns, fur coats, costume jewelry, vests, sweaters, hats, *occhiali da sole* (sunglasses), and men's suits are on display here, all in excellent condition. If needed, the shop can make alterations.

46

PUGI

PIAZZA SAN MARCO 10

☎ 055 280981 · *focacceria-pugi.it*

MON–SAT 7:45AM–8PM;

CLOSED SUN

THE EVER-CONSTANT THRONG OF FLOREN-TINES WAITING FOR THEIR FAVORITE focaccia to emerge from the oven is a testament to Pugi's genius. A local institution, this bakery creates sublime pizza, focaccia, and *schiacciata* in every imaginable combination: plain, stuffed, or topped with vegetables, meat, and cheese, and in autumn,

with wine grapes, sugar, and fennel seed. Pugi stays in step with the seasons, baking traditional holiday sweets: *frittelle* (sweet rice fritters) for the feast of San Giuseppe, *cenci* for Carnevale, *pan ramerino* for Lent, and panettone at Christmas. You can eat standing up, or they will wrap it for you (but who can wait?) Pugi also carries delicious *torte di frutta* and *biscotti di Prato*.

47

MAISON ROUGE

VIA CAVOUR 82R

▭ ☎ 055 280342

MON—SAT 10AM—6:30PM;

CLOSED SUN

MAISON ROUGE'S SIGNATURE BLOUSES, DRESSES, SWEATERS, SKIRTS, AND JACKETS are lush, romantic fashions evocative of another era: irresistible, ornate combinations of lace, linen, chenille, and velvet in Victorian styles that are ultrafeminine yet exceedingly comfortable.

All garments are handmade in Italy, from winter confections of velvet to spring and summer dresses of delicate embroidered pastel linen with lace.

48

DREONI

VIA CAVOUR 31/33R

☎ 055 216611 · *dreoni.it*

MON 3:30−7:30PM;

TUE−SAT 10AM−7:30PM; CLOSED SUN;

CLOSED SAT AFTERNOON IN AUG

THREE GENERATIONS OF DREONIS HAVE CHARMED THREE GENERATIONS OF FLOREN-tines, who continue to bring their children into this enchanted wonderland, filled floor to ceiling with every toy conceivable: trains, planes, cars (the classic Fiat Cinquecento, in miniature, below), stuffed animals, dolls of all persuasions, knights, soldiers, puzzles, educational toys, construction sets, kites, costumes, masks, and musical games. Select a Pinocchio from two inches to six feet tall (the larger ones come with several nose lengths that can be changed according to the magnitude of the lie). Even the cash register is playful: one side features a nearly life-size train and the other side a colorful gingerbread house.

CARABÉ
Via Ricasoli 60r 🚫 ☎ 055 289476
9am–1am daily · Inexpensive

The Sicilian owners, emphatic about using only seasonal ingredients, make superb fruit- and nut-flavored gelato. For a breakfast you'll never forget, order the coffee granita with whipped cream and a brioche. You won't see cannoli on display, as they are made to order, but they are worth asking for.

Ⓨ
ARÀ
Via degli Alfani 127r 🚫 ☎ 328 6117029
10am–10pm daily · Moderate

A bright, modern oasis of deliciously beautiful Sicilian specialties: *arancini* (rice balls with different savory fillings) and *pizzole* (small, just-baked pizzas sliced in half, stuffed with a choice of fillings). Save room for a delectable sweet: *cassata* made with ricotta, almond paste, and candied orange peel, or biscotti with chocolate from Modica. Arà also carries a fine list of wines by the glass. Seating is limited.

ROBIGLIO

Via dei Servi 112r ▭ ☎ 055 212784
Mon–Sat 8am–8pm; closed Sun & Aug
Moderate

This is a good option at any time of day: have a light lunch or a salad, quiche, or panino, or savor a cappuccino and freshly made *torta* at this classic Florentine pasticceria, founded in 1928. Robiglio's proximity to the University of Florence guarantees that at commencement time you will spot relieved college graduates sporting congratulatory laurel wreaths, sipping *spumante* with friends and family.

PUGI

Piazza San Marco 10
⧸ ☎ 055 280981 · *focacceria-pugi.it*
Mon–Sat 7:45am–8pm; closed Sun · Inexpensive
(see shop 47, p. 122)

RISTORANTE DA MIMMO
Via San Gallo 57/59r ▭ ☎ 055 481030
Mon–Fri lunch & dinner; Sat & Sun dinner only
Moderate

Housed in a former theater, with a dramatic frescoed ceiling from the seventeenth century, Ristorante da Mimmo is well loved by locals for always-fresh cuisine and quick, cheerful service. At lunch, the ever-changing *menù del lavoratore* (worker's menu) offers a choice of pastas, *insalatone* (big salads), and main courses at very reasonable prices. Order the *porchetta* (stuffed and rolled suckling pig), and Mimmo himself will slice it for you at your table.

At dinner, the full menu comes out and the tariff goes up, but a memorable dining experience is still ensured.

Piazza del Duomo

Via dello Studio

Via Sant'Egidio

55

Via dell'Oriuolo

Borgo Pinti

Via Fiesolana

Via di Mezzo

Via del Corso

Borgo degli Albizi

Via del Proconsolo

Via del Seggiole

54

Via de' Pandolfini

Via dell'Ulivo

Badia
Fiorentina

Via Ghibellina

h g

53

Via M. Palmieri

Via dell'Agnolo

49

e f

52

Via della Vigna Vecchia

Via delle Stinche

Piazza della
Signoria

Piazza
San
Firenze

Via della Burella

Via delle Pentole

Via Giuseppe Verdi

Via de' Pepi

Via M. Buonarroti

Borgo Allegri

Via del Gondi

Via dell' Anguillara

Piazza
Santa Croce

Via della Mattonaia

Via Ghibellina

Via San Cristofano

Via delle Pinzochere

Borgo de' Greci

Via de' Leoni

Via Lambertesca

Piazza dei
Peruzzi

50

Via de' Neri

Via delle Brache

Via de' Benci

Santa Croce

Via San Giuseppe

c d

Borgo Santa Croce

Via Magliabechi

Piazza
Mentana

Via dei Vagellai

51

Corso dei Tintori

Lungarno Generale A. Diaz

Piazza dei
Cavalleggeri

Via Tripoli

Lungarno delle Grazie

Ponte alle Grazie

FIUME ARNO

Lungarno Torrigiani

Giardino
di Palazzo
Serristori

Lungarno Serristori

Via de' Bardi

Via di San Niccolò

SHOPS

(49) I Fiori della Signoria al Portico

(50) Jamie Marie Lazzara

(51) Aqua Flor

(52) Filistrucchi

(53) Libreria Salimbeni

(54) Vestri

(55) Sbigoli Terrecotte

FOOD & DRINK

(c) Gelateria dei Neri

(d) Brac

(e) Vivoli

(f) Osteria Caffè Italiano

(g) Pizzeria dell'Osteria del Caffè Italiano

(h) Sud

I FIORI DELLA SIGNORIA AL PORTICO

PIAZZA DELLA SIGNORIA 37R

☎ 055 2608658 · *semialportico.it*

MON–SAT 8:30AM–8PM; SUN 10AM–2PM

FOR CLOSE TO FIFTY YEARS, THIS URBAN OASIS IN A LIGHT-FILLED FORMER CONVENT HAS been supplying everything for the gardening enthusiast: beautiful flowering plants (including gardenias year-round), bulbs, terra-cotta pots, even *pezzi di David* (facsimile fragments of Michelangelo's famous statue). Seductively packaged seeds of every variety are hard to pass up, green thumb or not. If you choose to purchase cut flowers as a gift, charming *proprietaria* Maurizia Venturi will be happy to advise you on the best way to make a *bella figura*.

50

JAMIE MARIE LAZZARA

VIA DEI LEONI 4R

✆ 055 280573

MON–FRI 9:30AM–1PM & 3–7PM;

SAT BY APPT; CLOSED SUN

ONE IS HESITANT TO DISTURB JAMIE MARIE LAZZARA AS SHE PAINSTAKINGLY WORKS IN the silence of her tiny shop filled with violin parts. A prodigy at the age of eight, she came to Italy over three decades ago to study violin making. Now a *Maestro Liutaio*, as her classic gold-leaf sign proclaims, Lazzara creates and repairs violins and violas for many celebrated musicians. She is especially proud to have crafted Itzhak Perlman's first modern instrument, which he played at Barack Obama's presidential inauguration and which led to Lazzara's commission to make yet another violin— this time for Malia Obama. Her small workstation holds a stack of press clippings about this event.

Director Ridley Scott was so taken with Lazzara's shop that it inspired a scene in his 2001 film *Hannibal*, which was shot in Florence.

51

AQUA FLOR

BORGO SANTA CROCE 6

▭ ☎ 055 2343471 · *florenceparfum.com*

MON–SUN 10AM–7PM

ENTER THIS HISTORIC PALAZZO TO FIND *PRO-FUMERIA* AQUA FLOR'S VAST, AIRY SPACE WITH vaulted ceilings and glass-fronted, dark carved wood cabinets. Master perfumer Sileno Cheloni creates limited-edition fragrances from obscure ingredients—such as Himalayan musk and Damascus rose—that he travels the world to collect. There are so many fragrances to choose from, it is recommended that you pause to take a whiff from a glass goblet of espresso beans to clear the nose. Should you prefer your own personal fragrance, Cheloni will be happy to consult with you for two to three hours to determine your perfect scent. Cheloni's favorite? "Whatever I'm currently working on," he answers, although he admits that he never travels without a tiny bottle of pure rose essence.

52

FILISTRUCCHI

VIA GIUSEPPE VERDI 9

☎ 055 2344901 · *filistrucchi.it*

MON 3–7PM; TUE–FRI 8:30AM–12:30PM & 3–7PM;

SAT 8:30AM–12:30PM;

CLOSED SUN & AUG

FILISTRUCCHI IS A LEADING EXPERT IN THE PRODUCTION OF HUMAN-HAIR WIGS AND BEARDS, papier-mâché masks, makeup, and special effects for film, theater, and television. The business has flourished in the same location, under the direction of the same family, since 1720. Although it has survived two major floods (in 1844 and 1966), the interior has remained virtually intact. All work is done on the premises, in the upstairs laboratory.

While both father and son respectfully decline to name names, it is clear that their clients include internationally renowned actors and actresses.

53

LIBRERIA SALIMBENI

VIA M. PALMIERI 14/16R

▭ ☎ 055 2340904 · *libreriasalimbeni.com*

MON—SAT 10AM—1PM & 4–7:30PM; CLOSED SUN

FROM ITS MODEST BEGINNINGS IN 1940 AS A SCRAP PAPER STORE, LIBRERIA SALIMBENI IS today one of the most highly regarded bookstores for art and antiquarian subjects. In 1966 Salimbeni launched its own publishing company, although the first book suffered an untimely debut just days before a historic flood devastated Florence. The imprint continued through the 1990s to publish several notable facsimile editions of Futurist books and periodicals, many of which are still available.

Today, the second generation of Salimbeni, siblings Serenella and Stefano, continue the family tradition by offering an impressive catalog (also available online) and expert service.

54

VESTRI

BORGO DEGLI ALBIZI 11R

☎ 055 2340374 · *vestri.it*

MON–SAT 10:30AM–8PM; CLOSED SUN & AUG

Advice to a chocoholic visiting Florence: choose a hotel as close as possible to Vestri, on the Borgo degli Albizi.

Made in Arezzo laboratories in copper pots, these intense artisan chocolates flavored with chili pepper, nuts, apricots, oranges, or espresso are truly addictive. Florentines look forward to warmer weather, when Vestri's creamy, dreamy, chocolate gelato spiked with mint, cayenne, hazelnut, and other enticing flavors is hand-scooped by Leonardo Vestri himself. For the ultimate indulgence, try a shot of sumptuous *cioccolato da bere* (drinkable chocolate)—hot in winter, cold in summer, and always delicious.

55

SBIGOLI TERRECOTTE

VIA SANT'EGIDIO 4R

☎ 055 2479713 · *sbigoliterrecotte.it*

MON–SAT 9AM–1PM & 2:30–7:30PM; CLOSED SUN

ORIGINALLY FOUNDED IN 1857 AND A FAMILY OPERATION SINCE 1966, SBIGOLI features beautiful Tuscan handpainted terra-cotta in traditional as well as contemporary designs. The spacious shop is a colorful extravaganza of gaily decorated plates, urns, pitchers, serving pieces, tea and espresso sets, custom signs, house numbers, lamps, sundials, terra-cotta-topped tables on wrought-iron bases, glazed earthenware cooking pots, and unglazed pots for the garden or terrace. Antonella Adami, born into a family of ceramicists, and her daughter Lorenza, at work at the back of the shop, will help you select and ship home the perfect piece of pottery.

[144]

(c)

GELATERIA DEI NERI
Via dei Neri 9/11r ∌ ☎ 055 210034
11am–midnight daily · Inexpensive

Excellent gelato and sorbetto, with a selection of *soia* (soy) flavors. Try the intense dark chocolate without milk, the intriguing ricotta and fig, the wild strawberry, or the namesake flavor for Florentine painter and architect Giotto (coconut and almond). The ever-patient staff is always helpful with the often-indecisive customer.

(d)

BRAC
Via dei Vagellai 18r
▭ ☎ 055 0944877 · *libreriabrac.net*
Mon–Sat 10am–midnight; Sun noon–midnight · Moderate

This unique literary caffè is a breath of fresh air in a city that at times takes itself and its local cuisine too seriously. Brac's small, signless door on Via dei Vagellai can be easy to miss. Once inside, you will be greeted by a vibrant decor of posters and sculptures, an open courtyard bedecked with long, colorful strips of cloth, and a dining room lined with shelves of contemporary art books and twinkling candles. The vegetarian/vegan menu is inspired and delicious, with wines by

the glass given as much description as the food. Order the *tris* and compose your own combination plate of three selections. Brac serves breakfast, lunch, and dinner well into the night. The kitchen is small, so do not expect speedy service, but you'll have plenty of reading matter. Reserve ahead.

VIVOLI
Via Isola delle Stinche 7r

🚫 ☎ 055 292334 · *vivoli.it*

Tue–Sun 8am–1am; closed Mon · Inexpensive

Family-owned Vivoli has been one of Florence's best-loved gelaterias since 1930. Follow the trail of discarded cups (no cones here) along Via Isola delle Stinche and try the dark chocolate with bitter orange or caramelized pear. The *affogato*—hot espresso poured over vanilla gelato in a pre-chilled cup—is drinkable perfection.

OSTERIA CAFFÈ ITALIANO
Via Isola delle Stinche 11r ▭ ☎ 055 289368

Lunch & dinner Tue–Sun; closed Mon · Moderate

With its vaulted ceiling, wrought-iron chandelier, and dark wood paneling, this is an ideal place to savor Tuscan specialties with a glass of excellent local wine. While lunch is reasonably priced, dinner requires deeper pockets.

Caffè Italiano offers two other options for evening meals: a few doors north, the tiny PIZZERIA DELL'OSTERIA DEL CAFFÈ ITALIANO ⓖ makes three kinds of pizza in a wood-burning oven: Margherita, Napoli, and marinara. No frills. No smiles. Great pizza. Seven euros. Cash only. Eat in if you find space at one of the six benches, or take away (at one euro less) and enjoy in nearby Piazza Santa Croce. 7:30pm–midnight; open daily (closed Mon, Nov–Feb).

Around the corner is SUD ⓗ (Via della Vigna Vecchia 4; Tues–Sun 7:30–11:00pm), featuring the cooking of southern Italy. Tables are set around a large glass case filled with sun-dried tomatoes, anchovies, caponata, *taralli*, focaccia stuffed with potatoes, and typical southern cakes and cookies. Try *fave e cicoria* or the freshly made *orecchiette* or *cavatelli*.

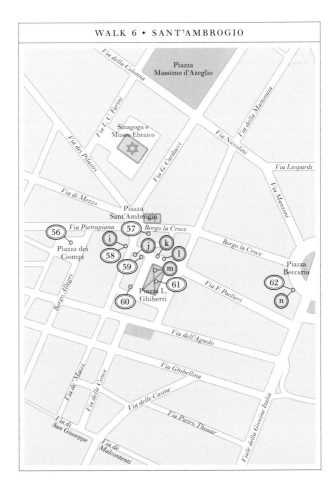

SHOPS

56 Mercato delle Pulci

57 Mesticheria Mazzanti

58 Cibreo Teatro del Sale

59 Lisa Corti

60 Angela Salamone

61 Mercato di Sant'Ambrogio

62 Dolci & Dolcezze

FOOD & DRINK

(i) Cibreo Teatro del Sale

(j) Caffè Cibreo

(k) Gilda

(l) Semel

(m) Trattoria da Rocco

(n) Dolci & Dolcezze

MERCATO DELLE PULCI

PIAZZA DEI CIOMPI

≠ TUE–SAT 10AM–7PM;

LAST SUN OF THE MONTH (EXCEPT JUL) 10AM-7PM;

CLOSED MON

THIS SLEEPY LITTLE FLEA MARKET CONSISTING OF TWENTY-FOUR DEALERS IS OPEN ALL DAY (no midday closing) and is located in the Piazza dei Ciompi, named after the woolworkers of medieval Florence. Everything from genuine antiques to pure junk can be unearthed here: vintage tins, buttons, photographs, jewelry, books, postcards, lace, perfume bottles, light fixtures, and tools. It is hard to leave without at least one new find, and, if nothing else, the relaxed attitude of the dealers can be refreshing. On the last Sunday of the month (except July), the market spills into the entire piazza, with nearly one hundred dealers, affording more exciting prospects.

BORGO LA CROCE 101R

≠ ☎ 055 2480663

MON—SAT 8AM—1PM & 3:30—7:30PM;

CLOSED SUN & AUG

THE TRANSLATION OF *MESTICHERIA* (HARD-WARE STORE) DOES NOT DO JUSTICE TO this shop, a celebration of all things for the everyday household. Room after room is jam-packed with brightly colored dishcloths, festively patterned cheesecloth by the meter, wineglasses, espresso cups, and glazed terra-cotta pots for oven or stovetop cooking. Disposable placemats made from *carta paglia* (a rough ocher-colored paper once used in butcher shops) are easy to roll up and take home. In summer, you'll find practical items such as innovative mosquito repellents and *coprifrutta a rete*, a three-tiered netted cage to protect fruit from unwanted visitors.

VIA DE' MACCI 111R

▭ ☎ 055 2001492 · *teatrodelsale.com*

TUE–SAT BREAKFAST, LUNCH & DINNER;
CLOSED SUN, MON & AUG

IN A CITY OF SO MANY OPINIONS, PARTICULARLY WHEN IT COMES TO FOOD, EVERYONE SEEMS TO be in agreement that Fabio Picchi of Cibreo is a visionary chef/restaurateur. He has transformed a tiny neighborhood near the Mercato di Sant'Ambrogio, east of Santa Croce, into nothing less than an empire of Florentine cuisine. Picchi demurs: "*Non è un impero—è una città!*" (It's not an empire—it's a city!)

The most recent addition to his already legendary restaurant, trattoria, and caffè is Cibreo Teatro del Sale—a private club housed in a cavernous fourteenth-century former convent. For a mere seven euros, one can become a *socio* (member), signing a contract to abide by the rules. Membership privileges include breakfast, lunch, and dinner at very reasonable prices. Dinner features a live performance, in addition to Picchi's in the kitchen,

neither of which should be missed. The shop, which greets you at the entrance to the theater and is open to members and nonmembers alike, sells a variety of carefully selected products, from Cibreo's own preserved vegetables and *marmellate* to pâtés, carnaroli rice, honey from the isle of Elba, bath products by Lorenzo Villoresi, and local wines. Look for Cibreo's signature *bicchieri riciclati* (recycled drinking glasses). Cut down from wine bottles and used in the restaurant, they are a bargain at four euros each. (Or spring for the gift box of eight for thirty euros.)

Once you purchase your membership card, make a reservation for dinner, which starts promptly at 7:30pm. Picchi, working with his staff in the massive, glassed-in kitchen, prepares course after course, dramatically announcing each as it is sent to the buffet table: "*Risotto del Principe!*" He will holler out suggestions as well: Don't eat too much bread; don't mix your salad with the rest of the food on your plate; pace yourself. Best of all, pasta dishes, which do not appear on the menu in his other restaurants, are here in full force. After an unforgettable meal (followed by squares of flourless chocolate cake), the kitchen blinds are drawn, chairs turn toward the stage, and the evening's entertainment begins—anything from a string quartet to an accordion band—arranged by Picchi's wife, Maria Cassi, who often performs her own hilarious monologues.

A visit to Florence is not complete without a trip to the *città* of Cibreo.

59

LISA CORTI

PIAZZA L. GHIBERTI 33R

☎ 055 2001860 · *lisacortifirenzeroma.com*

MON 3–7:30PM

TUE–SAT 10AM–1:30PM & 3:30–7:30PM;

CLOSED SUN & AUG

LISA CORTI'S BRIGHT AND AIRY SHOP NEAR THE SANT'AMBROGIO MARKET IS A CELEBRATION of color and pattern, owing to this Italian designer's childhood in Africa, with frequent trips to India and Southeast Asia. Corti's unique line of all-natural block-printed cottons, organzas, and fine muslins includes quilts, bedspreads, curtains, tablecloths, pillow covers, placemats, lampshades, and even smartphone covers in boldly delicious floral and geometric motifs, all printed in India. The same fabrics are crafted into comfortable clothing for women and children.

60

ANGELA SALAMONE

PIAZZA L. GHIBERTI 16R

▭ ☎ 339 7025562

MON 10AM–1PM; TUE–FRI 10AM–1PM; 2:30–7PM

SAT 10AM–2PM;

CLOSED SUN & AUG

THE NORWEGIAN-SICILIAN ANGELA SALAMONE BRINGS NEW LIFE TO THE ART OF TRADItional bookbinding with her line of modernist albums, notebooks, frames, folders, and portfolios created from paper, cotton, and linen. In this tiny, light-filled corner shop opposite the Sant'Ambrogio market, the soft-spoken Salamone, who studied both art and philosophy in Florence, creates meticulously crafted pieces in brilliant hues of fuchsia, tangerine, and lavender, using a combination of traditional Italian and Japanese techniques.

Allow extra time for gift wrapping, which in Salamone's hands is an art in itself.

61

MERCATO DI SANT'AMBROGIO

≠ PIAZZA L. GHIBERTI

MON—SAT 7:30AM—1:30PM; CLOSED SUN

THE SANT'AMBROGIO MARKET'S INTIMATE SCALE AND EXCELLENT PRODUCE MAKE IT a favorite among every generation of Florentines, who flock each morning to the Piazza Ghiberti with their oversized shopping totes.

The bustling outdoor section features tantalizing pyramids of beautifully displayed fruits and vegetables of the season. The sellers are equally courteous whether you buy one apple or carry away a kilo. It can often appear that the vendors' survival depends on their ability to outshout their rivals, with earnest cries of *"Freschissimo!"* (The freshest!) or *"Bellissimi!"* (The most beautiful!). The edibles are juxtaposed with a cheerful hodgepodge of constantly changing wares: clothing, intimate apparel, shoes, baby clothes, table linens, household items, kitchen gadgets, notions, and cut flowers—all at extremely reasonable prices. Step inside the airy, hangarlike interior (where you will be greeted

by a large mosaic Florentine lily on the floor) for an enticing sprawl of stands selling all types of meats (heads, tails, crests, and innards included) and many varieties of fresh and aged cheeses, prosciuttos, salamis, breads, honey, fresh and dried pastas, grains, beans, eggs, olives, spices, sauces, oils, fresh and salted fish, milk, yogurt, and coffee, as well as a caffè and a trattoria (see page 171).

The *mercato* gets high marks for conveniences; clean bathrooms are available downstairs for sixty *centesimi*, and bike rentals can be arranged at the far end of the market (between the flower stalls and the parking garage) by the hour or by the day.

62

DOLCI & DOLCEZZE

PIAZZA BECCARIA 8R

🚫 ☎ 055 2345458 · *dolciedolcezzepasticceria.it*

TUE–SAT 8:30AM–8PM;

SUN 9AM–1PM & 4:30–7:30PM;

CLOSED MON

I N THE LOVELY, LESS TOURIST-TRAVELED PIAZZA BECCARIA, DOLCI & DOLCEZZE IS AS ARRESTING to the eye as it is to the palate. With an elegant mint-lacquered facade and strikingly beautiful interior of oil paintings, crystal chandeliers, and inlaid marble floor, this diminutive pasticceria presents a signature flourless chocolate cake and delicious fresh fruit tarts, along with a selection of equally intriguing savories.

Having had no professional training, just a passion for inventive baking, Ilaria Ballatresi started the shop with her husband, Giulio, thirty-three years ago. Since his death, she has maintained the business with her two children, exacting the same high standards: using traditional, time-honored recipes handed down from generations and only the best-quality artisan ingredients, in season. In

more recent years, Balatresi has focused on organic and all-natural ingredients.

In winter, look for *marrons glacés* and chocolates, and in summer, magical confections made with all seasonal fruits. Stand at the bar and enjoy a cappuccino or hot chocolate served in a fine white china cup while contemplating the shelves of beautifully displayed *marmellate*, *gianduja*, and biscotti.

It would be difficult to leave Dolci & Dolcezze without taking note of the plaque that states, "*Sono la torta alla cioccolata più buona del mondo.*" (I am the world's best chocolate cake.) This is no exaggeration. The cake can be "*personalizzata*" with whatever words or imagery that you fancy.

On weekdays, Dolci & Dolcezze is open all day to accommodate your sweet or savory craving.

WALK 6 ✦ FOOD & DRINK

(i) **CIBREO TEATRO DEL SALE**
Via de' Macci 111r 💳 ☎ 055 2001492
teatrodelsale.com
Breakfast, lunch & dinner Tue–Sat; closed Sun, Mon & Aug
(Reservations required for dinner) · Moderate
(see shop 59, p. 154)

(j) **CAFFÈ CIBREO**
Via Andrea del Verrocchio 5r 💳 ☎ 055 234 5853
Tue–Sat 8am–midnight; Sun 8:30am–7pm; closed Mon;
Moderate

Looking for the same sublime Cibreo experience but don't have time for a long lunch? Inside the coffered-ceilinged Caffè Cibreo you will revel in the heavenly pastries, flavorful little sandwiches (chicken salad, anchovy, and prosciutto), or, at lunchtime, tastes from the restaurant's daily specials, along with wines and Prosecco offered by the glass. Any time of day is the right time for barman Isidoro's legendary espresso and cappuccino. Weather permitting, enjoy your breakfast or lunch at an outside table while watching Florentines head to and from the Sant'Ambrogio market.

(k) **GILDA**
Piazza L. Ghiberti 40/41r 💳 ☎ 055 2343885
Breakfast, lunch & dinner; closed Sun · Moderate

This small, eclectic bistro's proximity to the Sant'Ambrogio market ensures fresh, seasonal dishes that are delicious and reasonably priced. Reservation notwithstanding, you may have to wait for a table, in which case the *elegante* Gilda will set you up at the bar, where you can enjoy the lively local scene while savoring a dish of polenta with a golden baroque goblet of white wine.

SEMEL
Piazza L. Ghiberti 44   🚫   *no phone*
Mon–Sat 11:30am–3pm; closed Sun & Aug · Inexpensive

Semel offers delicious artisan panini and classical music in an intimate setting, where you will be greeted by a smiling *proprietario*/Sean Connery doppelgänger. Whether duck breast, roasted pork, donkey stew, or marinated sardines (or the more prosaic vegetarian or classic cheese and salami), each panino is layered with innovative seasonings, sauces, and vegetables and served on a freshly baked roll. Artisan beer and selected wines are offered by the glass. There are five spots to perch at the counter; otherwise you can take away.

TRATTORIA DA ROCCO
Inside the Mercato di Sant'Ambrogio, Piazza L. Ghiberti
🚫   ☎   339 8384555 · *Mon–Sat noon–3pm; closed Sun;*
Inexpensive

Fresh, good, cheap, and fast is what you will find at this simple lunch spot in the bustling market. *Primi piatti* such as *pappa al pomodoro* and *lasagne alla genovese* are priced at four euros; *secondi* (*pollo arrosto, melanzana ripiena*) are only five euros.

DOLCI & DOLCEZZE ⓝ
Piazza Beccaria 8r   🚋   ☎   055 2345458
Tue–Sat 8:30am–8pm; Sun 9am–1pm & 4:30–7:30pm;
closed Mon · Moderate
(see shop 63, p. 166)

Standing room only, but who cares when you are experiencing the world's best chocolate cake?

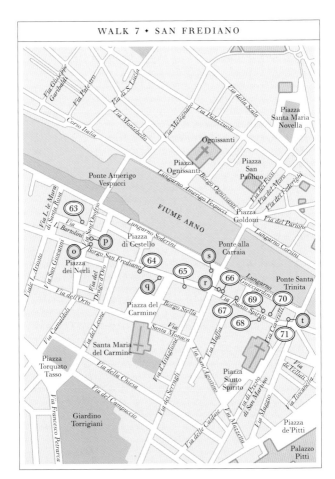

SHOPS

(63) Antico Setificio
Fiorentino

(64) Il Paralume

(65) Twisted

(66) Francesco da Firenze

(67) Quelle Tre

(68) Castorina

(69) Studio Puck

(70) Fiorile

(71) Olio & Convivium

FOOD & DRINK

(o) Angolo Saporito

(p) All'Antico Ristori di
Cambi

(q) Trattoria del Carmine

(r) Il Santo Bevitore

(s) Gelateria la Carraia

(t) Olio & Convivium

ANTICO SETIFICIO FIORENTINO

VIA L. BARTOLINI 4

☎ 055 213861 · *anticosetificiofiorentino.it*

MON—FRI BY APPT;

CLOSED SAT, SUN & AUG

O N VIA BARTOLINI, LOOK FOR A WROUGHT-
IRON GATE AND A NUMBER FOUR THAT IS
neither red nor black. (There is actually a sign for
Antico Setificio Fiorentino, though it is partially
obscured by climbing vines.)
Ring the bell under number four,
and walk straight ahead to another
gate, where you will be buzzed in to
another century.

An idyllic, leafy green courtyard is silent except for the sound of
swallows and the rhythmical hum
of the original eighteenth-century
looms from the adjacent *laboratorio*.
You have just walked into one of the
last remaining silk manufactur-
ing workshops in the world. Inside

the showroom, bolts of colorful, shimmering silks, brilliant damasks, and opulent brocades fill room after room. *Ermisino*, a particular type of taffeta that glows with subtle iridescence, is woven exclusively here. This and other signature fabrics such as *broccato* (pure silk and yarn), *damasco* (damask broccato), *filaticcio* (an ancient silk and linen cloth), *lampasso*, Le Roy (named in honor of the king of France), and Nemours (named after the Duke of Nemours, son of Lorenzo the Magnificent) are depicted in the Renaissance paintings of Masaccio, Bronzino, and Piero della Francesca.

While the Antico Setificio's list of clients can be intimidating (the Kremlin, the Royal Palaces of Stockholm, and the Quirinale in Rome), the curtains, bedspreads, silk and cashmere scarves, and bags filled with potpourri from the Officina Profumo Farmaceutica di Santa Maria Novella (page 64) will not break the bank. Silk-covered boxes and jewel cases, tassels, braids, pillows, picture frames, notebooks, and photo albums are also available in a variety of colors and styles.

Remember to call or write ahead to make an appointment at the *setificio*.

64

IL PARALUME

BORGO SAN FREDIANO 47

▭ ☎ 055 2396760 · *ilparalume.it*

MON–FRI 9AM–1PM & 3:30–7:30PM;

SAT 9AM–1PM; CLOSED SUN & AUG

FOR NEARLY SEVEN DECADES, IL PARALUME HAS BEEN PRODUCING LAMPS AND LAMPSHADES out of its labyrinthine workshop at the back of the store. Classic Florentine chandeliers, wall lamps, table lamps, tables, and mirrors are all made by hand, using only Italian materials. The hand-painted lamp bases are crafted from carved wood and metal and are either left natural, gold plated, or lacquered. The owner will proudly tell you that those are his lamps in the bar scenes in the film *La Dolce Vita*. Should you not find exactly what you are looking for in the hundreds of styles in both the workshop and the showroom across the street, it can be created for you, which will take about a week's time. Paralume ships worldwide.

65

TWISTED

BORGO SAN FREDIANO 21R

≠ ☎ 055 282011

MON—SAT 9AM—12:30PM & 3—7:30PM;

CLOSED SUN

STEFANO NUZZO'S TEN-YEAR-OLD SHOP ON BORGO SAN FREDIANO IS A HAVEN FOR ENTHU-siasts of film and jazz. New and used CDs, videos, DVDs, scores, books, posters, and postcards address all things jazz, from early, hard-to-find recordings to up-to-the-minute releases. Nuzzo is very enthusiastic about his impressive collection of vinyl recordings, and in his brightly lit, unadorned store, he will happily let you preview your selection in a listening station before you make your purchase.

Anime in delírio

JOAN CRAWFORD
VAN HEFLIN

...aciano di un amore inestinguibile

" Continua a baciarmi...
..., io continuerò a crederti!"

CON
RAYMOND MASSEY
GERALDINE BROOKS
In un film di
CURTIS BERNHARDT

VIA SANTO SPIRITO 62R

▭ ☎ 055 212428

MON–SAT 9AM–1PM & 3:30–7:30PM;

CLOSED SUN

B EHIND THIS BLINK-AND-YOU'LL-MISS-IT STOREFRONT YOU WILL DISCOVER THE workshop of Francesco Laudato, the source for classic and comfortable handmade leather shoes, sandals, boots, *sambi* (mules), and loafers for both men and women. Choose from his in-store stock or place a custom order: expect one month for a pair of shoes (which he can ship to you) or only a few days for sandals. Everything is made in the back of the shop by Francesco, who has been working at his craft since 1976, and his son Valerio (at right). Maestro and *figlio* now teach classes in the fine art of shoemaking.

67

QUELLE TRE

QUELLE TRE—THOSE THREE—BEAUTIFUL SISTERS HAVE BEEN MAKING INNOVATIVE clothes together for nearly three decades, using natural, high-quality fabrics—wool, cotton, linen, velvet, and corduroy—in warm earth and jewel tones. The soft-spoken sisters will help you select from jumpers, skirts, dresses, pants, jackets, vests, hats, gloves, scarves, and purses. A room dedicated to whimsical and colorful children's hats, baby blankets, stuffed toys, and dolls is a delight. Any item in the shop can be altered or specially ordered in your size or choice of color.

68

CASTORINA

VIA SANTO SPIRITO 15R

☎ 055 212885 · *castorina.net*

MON—FRI 9AM—1PM & 3—7PM; SAT 9AM—1PM;

CLOSED SUN & AUG

THE CASTORINA FAMILY, OF SICILIAN ORIGIN, HAS BEEN A LEADER IN WOOD CARVING since 1895. Their vast store is filled with an impressive array of moldings, columns, candlesticks, obelisks, trompe l'oeil tables, reading stands, mirrors and frames, angels and putti, goblets, vases, ornaments, fruit dishes and trays, globes, orbs, and lamp bases. All are available in an impressive selection of woods, finishes, and inlay patterns. While the sheer volume may be daunting, many of the smaller carved decorative elements (which Florentines use for furniture repair) can make distinctive souvenirs.

[188]

NB 311

TA 282/B

MA 106

TA 232/B

3E/30

382

MA 131

MA 16

TA 238

69

STUDIO PUCK

VIA SANTO SPIRITO 28R

☎ 055 280954 · *studiopuck.it*

MON–FRI 10AM–6PM; SAT 10AM–1PM;

CLOSED SUN & AUG

A RELATIVE NEWCOMER (TWENTY-FIVE YEARS) TO THIS HISTORIC NEIGHBORHOOD, Studio Puck (pronounced "Pook" by Italians) takes craftsmanship to new heights. This staggeringly beautiful showroom features fine engravings printed on nineteenth-century presses hand-

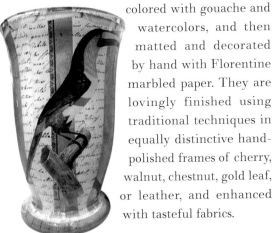

colored with gouache and watercolors, and then matted and decorated by hand with Florentine marbled paper. They are lovingly finished using traditional techniques in equally distinctive hand-polished frames of cherry, walnut, chestnut, gold leaf, or leather, and enhanced with tasteful fabrics.

70

FIORILE

VIA SANTO SPIRITO 26R

☎ 055 2049032 · *fiorile.it*

TUE–SAT 9:30AM–1:30PM & 3:30–7PM;

CLOSED SUN, MON & AUG

F IORILE CAN MAKE ANYTHING TO SUIT YOUR FLORAL NEEDS—FROM A TINY BOUQUET TO foliage for a grand wedding reception. This tasteful and unusual shop, filled not only with fragrant fresh flowers but also with vases, candles, lanterns, and a hundred other ideas for unique gifts to be used with or without blossoms, is a bright spot of greenery on the gray stone backdrop of Via Santo Spirito. *Naturalmente*, Fiorile's gift wrapping is as lovely and distinctive as the shop itself.

71

OLIO & CONVIVIUM

VIA SANTO SPIRITO 4

☎ 055 2658198 · *conviviumfirenze.it*

TUE–SUN 10AM–2:30PM & 5:30–10:30PM;

CLOSED MON

THE TILED FLOORS AND INVITING INTE-RIOR OF OLIO & CONVIVIUM PROVIDE A lovely respite along this street of workshops. Tuscan specialties of every variety are offered in this cheerful "gastronomic atelier" featuring arti-san breads, pastas, *salumi*, cheeses, and, of course, excellent extra-virgin olive oils. The *olioteca didat-tica* (oil tasting room) will turn anyone into a sated connoisseur. Cooking classes are given in the airy, open kitchen, and wine tasting seminars are held in the atelier.

The small adjacent restaurant is a perfect spot for an intimate lunch or elegant dinner.

(o) ANGOLO SAPORITO
Via Sant'Onofrio 7r 🚭 ☎ 370 3244149
Mon–Fri 7:30am–7:30pm; Sat 7:30am–1:30pm;
closed Sun & Aug · Inexpensive

Follow the fragrant aroma of freshly baked bread to this corner shop for *sbirulini* (bread sticks twisted with herbs or tomato), rolled bread baked with cheese and ham, or pizza sold by the slice, as well as all of the traditional holiday sweets baked throughout the year.

(p) ALL'ANTICO RISTORI DI CAMBI
Via Sant'Onofrio 1r 🍽 ☎ 055 217134
Mon–Sat noon–2:30pm & 6–10:30pm;
closed Sun & middle week of Aug · Moderate

This is consummate Florentine cooking. Since 1950 the Cambi family restaurant has been a fixture in the neighborhood, with a menu featuring traditional dishes such as *pappa al pomodoro*, *ribollita*, and pasta with boar sauce—all made the way *Mamma* would at home: fresh, flavorful, and with love. Specials change daily. Outdoor seating available.

 TRATTORIA DEL CARMINE
Piazza del Carmine 18r 🍽 ☎ 055 218601
Lunch & dinner daily; closed Sun Jun–Aug · Moderate

An institution for well over fifty years, this warm and welcoming family restaurant serves traditional Tuscan fare such as *bistecca fiorentina.* Choose from the ultrafresh daily specials (when artichokes are in season, the *insalata di carciofi* is superb). Good for people-watching, especially in warmer weather when outdoor seating is available.

IL SANTO BEVITORE

Via Santo Spirito 64/66r

▭ ☎ 055 211264 · *ilsantobevitore.com*

Lunch Mon–Fri; dinner Mon–Sat; closed Sun;
Moderate

In this spacious, inviting room with Renaissance vaulted ceilings, the creative, light lunch menu changes weekly, offering soups, pastas, and salads. Try the perfectly *al dente* spaghetti with mussels, sea bass, and cherry tomatoes or the cream of garbanzo bean soup doused with rosemary oil. The inspired dinner menu changes with the season. More than fifteen different wines are offered by the glass, as well as a tasting menu of wine, *vin santo*, and grappas.

GELATERIA LA CARRAIA

Piazza N. Sauro 25r ▱ ☎ 055 280695

11am–midnight daily; closed Jan · Inexpensive

Creamy gelato, friendly service, and reasonable prices give this conveniently located gelateria (named after the bridge it looks out on) a loyal following. Try the one-euro *cono degustazione*—a generously filled one-flavor "tasting" cone.

OLIO & CONVIVIUM

Via Santo Spirito 4

▭ ☎ 055 2658198 · *conviviumfirenze.it*

Mon 10am–3pm; Tue–Sat 10am–3pm & 5:30–10:30pm;
closed Sun (see shop 72, p. 194) · Moderate

A lovely spot for lunch, dinner, or an *aperitivo*. Excellent wines by the glass, along with cheeses, *salumi*, and oil tastings, are offered by a knowledgeable staff. Choose the bright-yellow room on the right as you enter, and watch the chefs busy at work in the kitchen.

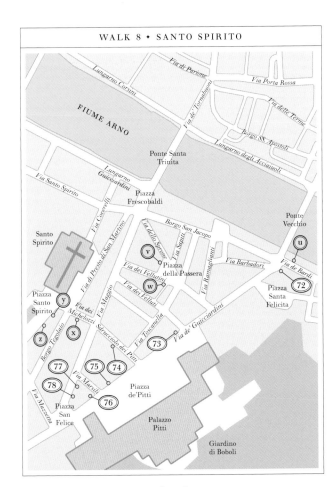

SHOPS

(72) Madova

(73) Giulio Giannini & Figlio

(74) Le Telerie Toscane

(75) Atelier

(76) Stile Biologico

(77) & Company

(78) Dolcissima Firenze

FOOD & DRINK

(u) Golden View Open Bar

(v) 5 e Cinque

(w) Trattoria 4 Leoni

(x) Trattoria la Casalinga

(y) Borgo Antico

(z) Caffè Ricchi

MADOVA

VIA DE' GUICCIARDINI 1R

▭ ☎ 055 2396526 · *madova.com*

MON–SAT 9:30AM–7:30PM;

CLOSED SUN; CLOSED SAT IN AUG

IN FLORENCE, *GUANTI* (GLOVES) ARE SYNON-YMOUS WITH MADOVA, SPECIALISTS IN THE field since 1919. Madova is proud to be the only shop in Europe that produces and sells leather gloves exclusively (making them in a factory just steps from the shop). These butter-soft gloves come in a spectrum of beautiful colors, with linings of silk, lambswool, or leather. Simply walk into the shop and present your hand, and Madova will do the rest. Without even having to measure, the expert staff will not only know what size you are but what type of leather, and in what color, will go best with what you are wearing. Of course, they are always correct.

73

GIULIO GIANNINI & FIGLIO

PIAZZA DE'PITTI 37R

☐ ☎ 055 212621 · *giuliogiannini.it*

MON–SAT 10AM–7:30PM; SUN 11AM–6:30PM

SINCE 1856, GIULIO GIANNINI & FIGLIO HAS BEEN A FAVORITE FOR ITS HANDMADE, QUINTES-sentially Florentine papers. Now under the direction of sixth-generation Maria Giannini, the shop is still the go-to destination for beautifully decorated papers and bound books. Located directly across the street from the Pitti Palace, Giannini carries blank books, journals, address books, stationery, cards, paper-wrapped pencils, bookplates, and frames, all in their distinctive patterns and all handmade in Florence.

Tiny blank books labeled *Oggetti dati in prestito* (things loaned) or *Compleanni* (birthdays) are also available in English and make charming gifts.

74

LE TELERIE TOSCANE

SDRUCCIOLO DEI PITTI 15R

☎ 055 216177 · *letelerietoscane.com*

TUE–SAT 10AM–1:30PM & 2:30–7PM;

CLOSED SUN & MON

TUCKED AWAY ON THIS TINY STREET THAT LEADS TO THE PITTI PALACE, LE TELERIE Toscane features traditional Tuscan table linens, including tablecloths, runners, placemats, and napkins, as well as bedsheets, duvet covers, coverlets, pillows, aprons, and dishcloths, all in exquisite printed and jacquard fabrics. Their exclusive designs include classic country motifs: hunting scenes, fruit baskets, poppies, olives, and grapevines. Although sophisticated and beautiful, the fabrics are meant to withstand daily use. One of the patterns is a replica of the tablecloth in Andrea del Castagno's *Last Supper*, painted in 1450, at the Cenacolo of St. Apollonia. If your table or bed happens to be a nontraditional size, they will be happy to design to fit and will ship to you. The brightly colored and patterned dish towels make an extremely portable gift to take home.

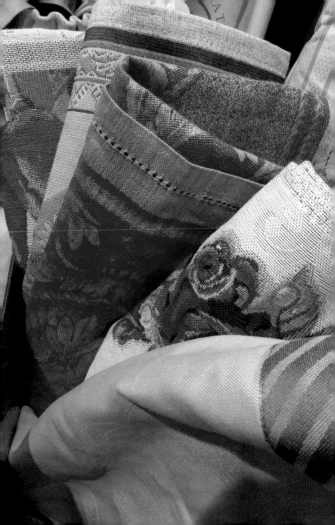

75

ATELIER

THE *SIMPATICO* ANTONIO GATTO, WHO COMES FROM A THEATER COSTUMING BACKGROUND, creates strikingly beautiful handcrafted hats for every occasion—made from straw, wool, linen, felt, and sisal—which are adorned with feathers, ribbons, buttons, and many of Gatto's vintage fabrics. The *cappellaio* also offers custom-made jackets and vests, "as the genius strikes me." This intimate space just across from the Pitti Palace does indeed feel like an atelier—stroll past rolls of fabric, spools of ribbon, paper patterns pinned on the walls, wooden hat forms, colored threads, and sewing machines to find Gatti quietly at work in the back of the shop.

76

STILE BIOLOGICO

PIAZZA DE'PITTI 6R

☎ 055 2776275 · *stilebiologico.it*

MON–SAT 10AM–7:30PM;

CLOSED SUN & AUG

A LEADER IN ENVIRONMENTALLY CONSCIOUS FASHION, GIUDITTA BLANDINI DESIGNS HER own line of beautiful and sophisticated clothing in *stile biologico*—using natural fibers that have not been chemically treated. Since 1997 her shop on the Piazza de'Pitti has featured simple and graceful sweaters, dresses, skirts, blouses, intimate apparel, shoes, hats, and children's clothes in lovely muted colors. These exceedingly comfortable yet stylish creations are fabricated in Tuscany from raw silk, hemp, alpaca, and lambswool, as well as organic cotton and linen, using only vegetable dyes. Ceramic and wool jewelry is also available.

[208]

77

& COMPANY

VIA MAGGIO 47R

☎ 055 219973 · *andcompanyshop.com*

TUE–SAT 10:30AM–1PM & 3–6:30PM;

CLOSED SUN & MON

BETTY SOLDI (A TUSCAN WHO SPENT THE BETTER PART OF HER LIFE IN LONDON) AND Matteo Perduca (a dyed-in-the-wool Florentine) offer a mix of the old and new in this intriguing shop: wood and metal type, vintage signs, graphic dinnerware, scarves, picture frames, and notecards. The paper cutouts (opposite) by twin Danish sisters are particularly enchanting. Across the street is Soldi's design studio, where she creates many of the calligraphic items found in the store and gives lettering workshops in her impeccable English.

78

DOLCISSIMA FIRENZE

VIA MAGGIO 61R

☎ 055 2396268 · *dolcissimafirenze.it*

TUE–SAT 9AM–1PM & 3:30–7:30PM;

SUN 9AM–1PM; CLOSED MON

THIS GLEAMING WHITE *LABORATORIO DI PASTICCERIA* LINED WITH CANDY-FILLED apothecary jars beckons to all passersby on Via Maggio. In the aptly named Dolcissima (very, very sweet), a crystal chandelier hovers gracefully over alluring glass cases of *torte* and biscotti that are almost too beautiful to eat. (But you must—the *torta di cioccolato fondente e peperoncino* and the custard and fresh fruit tarts are superb.) Dolcissima also carries dessert wines, *spumante*, liqueurs, grappas, and Sicilian *marmellate*, as well as a line of their own fine chocolates. Self-service Illy coffee is available from a machine in a discreet corner of the shop.

(u)
GOLDEN VIEW OPEN BAR
Via de Bardi 58r 🔲 ☎ 055 214502
Noon–midnight daily; pizza served until 1 am;
Moderate

Despite the curious name, Golden View Open Bar's airy rooms looking out onto the Arno make it an excellent spot for lunch, *aperitivo*, or dinner. Beautifully presented antipasti, salads, pizzas, and main courses are served just steps from the Ponte Vecchio. For dessert, head to Gelateria La Strega Nocciola across the street: Via dei Bardi 51r.

(v)
5 E CINQUE
Piazza della Passera 1 🔲 ☎ 055 2741583
Lunch & dinner; closed Sun and Mon · Moderate

The menu for this organic Ligurian restaurant changes daily according to what is in season. Satisfying pastas, risottos, soups, and *cecine* (chickpea pancakes) are served in a pleasant setting. Organic wines are available by the glass.

TRATTORIA 4 LEONI

Via dei Vellutini 1r ☎ 055 218562
Lunch & dinner; closed Wed lunch · Moderate

Trattoria 4 Leoni is the essential Tuscan kitchen, appealing to local artisans and divas alike. Try the *gran fritto dell'aia* (fried barnyard)—chicken, rabbit, zucchini, eggplant, potatoes, and polenta—or the deceptively simple *insalata della Passera* (cabbage, zucchini, avocado, *pinoli*). In summer, savor your meal outside in the tiny Piazza della Passera.

TRATTORIA LA CASALINGA

Via dei Michelozzi 9r ☎ 055 218624
Lunch & dinner; closed Sun & 3 weeks in Aug · Inexpensive

La Casalinga (the housewife) says it all: simple, satisfying homestyle cooking since 1961, with a menu that changes daily, in a boisterous setting. Prices are extremely reasonable.

BORGO ANTICO

Piazza Santo Spirito 6r ☎ 055 210437
Lunch & dinner; closed Mon · Moderate

Borgo Antico, where regulars come for excellent pizzas, risottos, and salads, is a good choice for an alfresco lunch or dinner on the Piazza Santo Spirito.

CAFFÈ RICCHI

Piazza Santo Spirito 9r ☎ 055 282173
Lunch & dinner; closed Sun · Moderate

Delicious pastas, pizzas, and composed salads at reasonable prices make Ricchi an ideal lunch spot, particularly in good weather, when you can sit outdoors and enjoy the quiet charm of Piazza Santo Spirito. Next door at number 8r is their restaurant, which is only open for dinner, and pricier.

AUTHORS' FAVORITES

INDEX BY SPECIALTY

INDEX BY NAME

ACKNOWLEDGMENTS

THE AUTHORS WOULD LIKE TO THANK ALL OF THE SHOP AND RESTAURANT PROPRIETORS WHO graciously took time from their busy schedules to be interviewed for this book. We are also grateful to Jennifer Lippert, Kevin Lippert, Sara Stemen at Princeton Architectural Press, as well as Tanya Heinrich, for their enthusiasm and support.

I am indebted to my staff, Kelly Thorn, Spencer Charles, and Nicholas Misani, for bringing this book to reality and to my family, Steven and Nicolas Heller, for their love and support. LF

Grazie to family and friends on both sides of the ocean and special appreciation to my *ragazzi*, Mario and Lorenzo Acciai, for doing the cooking while we were busy working. LA